COLOR ON COLOR

ELEGANT DESIGNS TO STITCH

COLOR ON COLOR

ELEGANT DESIGNS TO STITCH

JANET HAIGH

PHOTOGRAPHS BY JOHN HESELTINE

First published in 2004 by Coats Crafts UK Ltd.

First edition for North America published in 2005 by
Interweave Press, Inc.

Editor: Susan Berry
Design: Anne Wilson
Technical editor: Sally Harding
Illustrations: Janet Haigh
Photography: John Heseltine

All inquiries should be addressed to:
Interweave Press, Inc.
201 East Fourth Street
Loveland, CO 80537 USA
www.interweave.com

Conceived, edited, and designed for Coats Crafts UK Ltd. by
Berry & Co.
47 Crewys Road
Childs Hill
London NW2 2AU

Library of Congress Cataloging-in-Publication Data

Haigh, Janet.
  Color on color : elegant designs to stitch / Janet Haigh.
     p. cm.
  Includes index.
  ISBN 1-931499-85-3
  1. Embroidery--Patterns. 2. Fancy work. I. Title.
  TT771.H17 2005
  746.44'041--dc22
                              2004062496

10 9 8 7 6 5 4 3 2 1

CONTENTS

INTRODUCTION

Color has a direct and personal impact on all of us, whether we recognize it or not. We all have favorite colors—ones that we feel comfortable to wear, to paint our rooms with, or to choose for the flowers in our gardens. Some colors make us feel calm; pale blues, clear watery greens, and silvery grays are often chosen to promote soothing feelings, while reds and oranges are supposed to make us feel passionate and excited. We say, "I saw red" when we are describing sudden anger, and we also talk of feeling "blue" when we are sad.

Traditionally, in most cultures, there was a code or symbolism relating to color, but with the growth of information and interaction now possible between different cultures, the meanings are beginning to blur. In Christian-based cultures, for example, blue is for peace, white for purity, red for danger, yellow for jealousy, green for envy. However, in ancient China, yellow, the color of the sun, was the emperors' color and no one else was allowed to wear it. Royal purple is a color traditionally worn by western kings and queens, but this is surely a direct descendant of the exclusive use of Tyrean purple for the Roman emperors. This deep purple was made from the shells of crustaceans, and so rare and expensive to obtain that it was kept as a special color for the use of one person—death could result for anyone found wearing the color, because it was seen as an insult to the emperor.

So our attitudes to color are deeply rooted, both culturally and personally. However, I find that people are wary of using strong colors, both in their homes and for clothes, unless dictated by fashion. By using colors that you like, even in small proportions, you can really make a difference to your surroundings. Small splashes of color can make a neutral room look livelier. This book is full of projects that can be made to inject small spots of bright color into otherwise neutral color schemes, whether as a pillow or a picture frame, for example. The rich red and pink quilt could be embroidered for a baby, but could just as easily be transformed into a blue version if the old adage "pink for a girl, blue for a boy" holds sway!

The colors in the book are in themselves a personal choice: my own. So even though I am used to dealing with many different color "stories" and ranges for different design commissions, I still have my own preferences. People can recognize my work by the choice of colors and the way that I put them together. For instance, I prefer to work with rich pinks rather than strong reds, and generally opt for "in-between" colors: purplish blues, yellowy pinks, limy greens, turquoises, violets, and mauves.

If, however, you like stronger colors, you can start to put them together to make vibrant and striking combinations. A good way to start to identify colors that "work" for you is to flick through fashion and interior design magazines or even the pages of this book. Stop at the colors that you like and think about how you might define them. Are they bright or subtle, deep and rich, or pale and pretty? Do they look faded or fresh, jewel-bright, or softly muted? Get used to identifying the character of the colors that you like, then buy or make small items in them to wear or use in your home.

Easy ways to achieve successful color coordination for your home are to extract the colors for a chosen scheme or accessory from a favorite fabric, a rug, or even a bunch of flowers. The embroidered frames on pages 58–61 demonstrate a method of finding colors from any source by using scraps of paper (paint charts are good for this) that match the exact shade of the colors in the scheme. Place the scraps on top of, or next to, the actual color you are matching. All colors affect other colors, which is why designers and artists work in a white room or studio. Only when colors are seen against pure white or black can their true hue or quality be assessed. Using small bits of fabric and threads to play with in these simple embroidery projects is a quick and easy way to develop your own preferences. The wide range of colored embroidery threads available makes this craft one of the cheapest and easiest ways of experimenting with color. Although many of the projects here have recipes for color combinations, often with alternatives, this book isn't about color manipulation as such, but rather about trying out new color combinations.

UNDERSTANDING COLOR

When designing fabrics I prefer to think in terms of "rainbows" of color, rather than the primary and secondary color-wheel system so often used to define and describe color. The rainbow is, in fact, a ribbon of colors that blend into one another, made up of the three primary colors interspersed with the secondary colors: between yellow and red is orange, between yellow and blue is green and between blue and red comes purple. These "between" colors, known as secondary or tertiary colors, are made by blending the primary colors (red, yellow, and blue), which are so called because they are unable to be made from anything but themselves. When you start to mix the secondary or "between" colors together (the tertiary), the really interesting and subtle colors produced are my particular favorites.

A color harmony is produced easily by choosing one color—say, red—and using the colors on either side of it in the rainbow. This means that orange and red and yellow will combine together harmoniously, as will blue and purple and red. Harmonies can be soft or vibrant, and they will never appear to look uneasy or, for that matter, exciting.

If you want excitement, you should try placing opposite colors together—the colors opposite each other in the color circle (shown left in wool tapestry yarn). In this system, yellow is opposite purple and orange is opposite blue, so, if you put any of these opposing colors together, you will get some vibrant and lively combinations.

The colors in several of my projects have been inspired by an existing fabric; the bull's-eye cushion colors came from a favorite old Indian silk skirt of mine. But many other color schemes came about by playing with color harmonies and clashes, almost all starting with the rainbow as a guide.

I hope that the color combinations and the project ideas in this book give you the confidence to start building your own preferred color palette, rather than necessarily copying mine, and that they give you the opportunity to start trying out a new range of colors and styles in embroidery. Experiment and have fun!

Getting started

Having the right equipment for any job is essential for good work, and any handsewing will be easier and quicker with the correct needles, scissors, and embroidery frames. At the beginning of each project there is a check list of essential equipment, but it would be useful to assemble a few basic items before you start. The following is an explanation of the purpose they serve, and why you need them.

STITCHING EQUIPMENT

I would suggest that you equip yourself with the following basic items:

You need a box of stainless steel pins and a good range of needles. Buy a packet of assorted sizes of the following needle types: crewel embroidery needles are perfect for most types of embroidery because they have long eyes, for ease of threading thick threads, and sharp points; darning needles are useful for the heaviest threads; "sharps," the ordinary sewing needles with round eyes, can be used for general stitching. If you want to embroider with beads (see project on page 32), then a fine beading needle is a must.

Sharp scissors, in the right size and weight, are essential. Two pairs will do to start. A small pair of sharp-pointed embroidery scissors is useful for snipping off threads and for unpicking stitching when things go wrong. A pair of larger, dressmaker's shears (medium size) will be needed for cutting fabrics.

A fine steel thimble, although not essential, is useful if you really do a lot of embroidery. I didn't use one for years, and I still have the scars on the top of my finger to prove it.

You will also need a ruler or tape measure for calculating fabric sizes and cutting out.

Hoops and frames are valuable where the fabric needs to be stretched tight. Some embroidery cannot be worked successfully unless the ground fabric is taut. There are various special embroidery frames for this purpose, both round (hoop frames) and rectangular (stretcher frames), which come in a range of sizes. A medium-size hoop, for working on lightweight fabric, would be worth including in a basic kit, although many of the projects do not need to be stretched. A small stretcher frame—the straight-sided version of a hoop—is used for delicate fabrics because a hoop can leave an impression on a finely woven fabric. It is also useful for long strips of fabric that would get in your way if stretched in a hoop (see information on stretching embroidery on pages 90 and 91). I have lots of different sizes of hoops in my workroom, because they are lovely crafted wooden objects in themselves and very inexpensive to buy.

DESIGNING EQUIPMENT

You will also need some basic equipment for creating and transferring designs. A range of graph and tracing papers is useful, depending on the project being undertaken, as is a fabric marker to draw the design on the fabric to be embroidered. One item of equipment that I cannot do without is a water-soluble pen. Using it is the simplest way of transferring a design onto the embroidery fabric (see page 88); the blue mark that it makes washes out with cold water applied with a cloth or clean paintbrush, provided you remember not to iron the fabric first.

BASIC EQUIPMENT

Here are the basics you will need when starting to embroider—they are all available from Coats. Right (clockwise, from the top,): transfer, tracing, and graph papers; ruler; water-soluble pen and fabric-marking pencils; embroidery hoop; stainless steel pins and a selection of different sizes of embroidery and sewing needles; thimble; dressmaker's shears and small embroidery scissors; tape measure.

Choosing materials

The choice of fabrics and threads can make or mar your work. The following gives you some idea of the range at your disposal, but it is the marrying of the fabric color, weight, and texture with the appropriate thread, to suit the style and form of the chosen stitch, that will give your work a truly professional finish. You can, as I do, take your inspiration from a stitched sample and go on to create a project based on this form of embroidery, or you can have a design idea, then look for the ideal form of fabric, stitch, and thread to work it. Natural fabrics and threads always look and feel good to work with; where possible, choose these in preference to synthetics, unless you are looking for a very specific effect—a shiny rayon thread for the stitching on shisha mirrors, for example.

FABRICS & THREADS

You can embroider on a wide range of weights and types of fabric, and the type and structure of the weave will determine to some extent the embroidery designs you can employ. I have tried, in this book, to use a range of different fabrics and textures, as well as colors, because half of the pleasure in embroidery comes from experimenting with different stitches and varying effects. Those discussed here (and shown on pages 14–15) are just some of the fabrics I like and often use (and have used in this book). It is up to you to discover others!

Materials have been kept as simple as possible: fabrics that will show colors clearly and cleanly, and are easy to use, because this set of designs is aimed at a young market, with children and teens in mind as well as new homeowners. I have used a whole gamut of fabric colors—making up rainbows from red through oranges and yellows to greens, turquoises, blues, mauves, and purples, back to pinks and reds—and embellished them with embroidery stitches and beads.

Among the plain fabrics used in this book are felts, linens, cottons, and wools. Different fabric surfaces can dramatically affect the appearance of colors. Velvets or matte wool will make a color stronger, or even several shades deeper, depending on how the light catches it. A shiny or smooth cloth will make a color appear lighter. A voile or transparent fabric will render a color paler and more subtle.

Those new to embroidery do not always realize that you can embroider successfully on patterned fabrics as well as plain ones. Indeed, you can use embroidery to enhance an existing design, emphasizing one part of it with particular stitches or decorative embellishment (see the beaded bag on pages 32–35 and the bolster on pages 52–55). Apart from producing attractive, and very individual designs, it is a quick and easy way to produce a dramatically different effect. Among the patterned cotton fabrics, ginghams, stripes, and informal prints are all widely available and easy to care for.

For working counted thread stitches, you can purchase canvas or special counted-thread (evenweave) fabric (Aida) in a range of colors, and with different gauges. You will also need both backing fabrics (including iron-on adhesive ones) and a variety of lining fabrics, including batting for quilting.

As far as the threads are concerned, six-strand cotton embroidery floss, pearl cotton, and soft embroidery cotton all have a wide range of uses, while wool tapestry yarns are useful for thicker fabrics and more textured work, and are quick to stitch. Space-dyed (multicolored) threads add immediate variety and liveliness to the embroidery. Whether you choose to use threads that blend with the colors of the fabric or contrasting ones that emphasize it will depend on the style and nature of the design.

COLOR, FABRIC, AND STITCH

I always sample my designs first to test stitch types and thread weights and colors, and to check their suitability for the design in mind. Here are a few samples I did for the projects in this book so that you can see the range of colors and stitches on some very different fabrics. Samples of the fabrics, threads, and embellishments used are shown on pages 14 and 15.

SAMPLES OF MATERIALS

Shown here are some examples of the different weights and colors of fabrics and threads, as well as a few examples of the type of embellishments used for the principal embroideries in this book.

FABRICS

Right (clockwise, from top left): a range of plain, brightly colored felts suitable for embroidery; patterned cottons in which the pattern can be used as the inspiration for random embroidery; medium-weight tussah silk, natural woven linens, raw silk, and loosely woven linens in plain colors. In addition to the fabrics shown here, you will also need Aida counted-thread (evenweave) fabric (for the running-stitch frames on pages 58–61), which comes in various colors and gauges. You may also need lining, interfacing, batting, and backing fabrics in various weights and thicknesses.

THREADS

Right (clockwise, from center top): plain and multicolored pearl cotton, a shiny, twisted embroidery thread; a rayon thread; plain and multicolored six-strand cotton embroidery floss; soft embroidery cotton, a medium-weight matte thread; a wool tapestry-weight needlepoint yarn.

EMBELLISHMENTS

The following (shown right, center) are just some of the many different kinds of embellishment I use for my embroideries:
Beads: silver, clear glass, pearl, and iridescent, in shapes including round, rocailles, and bugle.
Shisha mirrors: clear, mirrored glass, and mirrors with embroidered edges in a range of colors.
Sequins: Various sizes in iridescent shades.

GALLERY OF PROJECTS

PATTERN DARNING

The inspiration for this embroidered flower design is from Mexico, where many textiles are made from darning stitches worked to look like a woven pattern. The use of variegated or space-dyed thread, which fades from dark to light to dark along the length of the thread, exploits the quality of this simple embroidery. The colors are very strong in Mexican work, because the embroiderers try to capture the vibrant shades of the native flowers. Roses are often worked in a stylistic way, but the colors are seldom natural.

Shaded strands of embroidery floss are essential for this technique, because they must form a flat wide stitch that covers the background easily. The floss is prepared by separating each individual strand from its neighbor before threading the needle; care needs to be taken to align the shading perfectly when reassembling the separated lengths.

I have chosen to work this design on a pair of brightly colored espadrilles, but you could use it on a bag or purse, on the corners of a napkin or tablecloth, or on the pocket of a kimono or shirt.

Mexican-style espadrilles

It is great fun to personalize a simple pair of inexpensive espadrilles. You can choose whatever thread colors take your fancy to make a strong contrast against the fabric color of the shoes. A flat, darned design like this one uses blocks of colors that create great graphic impact. I chose to use bright pinks, greens, blues, and yellows on a dark maroon shoe for bold contrast, but suggestions for other color combinations are given on page 23. You could use the design very easily, if you wished, for a small bag or purse.

HOW TO MAKE THE DESIGN

The design is embroidered onto the vamps of the shoes and has been carefully worked out so that it is possible to stitch the shapes in the limited space available. The darning stitches are easy and simple to work, but you need to start and finish the design with care (see the instructions on page 22). Variegated threads are ideal for this kind of design, but be sure to select ones that they have the greatest possible color variation.

MATERIALS

Pair of brightly colored espadrilles

One skein each of multicolor stranded cotton six-strand
  embroidery floss, in five bright, contrasting colors (Anchor
  used for model)

Darning needle, size 5

Water-soluble pen

Tracing paper

Dressmaker's carbon paper

Pencil

Embroidery scissors

Cardboard cut to fit inside the shoe

EMBROIDERING THE DESIGN

1 Trace the designs from page 108 onto tracing paper, drawing single lines along the stitching gaps. Put a piece of cardboard inside the espadrilles so that you can get a clear tracing of the motif when pressing hard on the back of a contrasting-colored dressmaker's carbon paper (see page 89 for transfer instructions). Place the lower edge of the motif no more than 2½" (6 cm) from the top edge of the espadrille, so you can stitch easily inside the vamp.

2 Mark the guidelines for the stitched areas using a blue water-soluble pen by drawing a line on each side of the original transfer line. This double line marks the gap in the stitching and makes an easy darning guide.

3 Cut a length of thread and separate the six strands of floss before threading the needle, making sure that each length has a good range of variegated color in it. Put the six strands back together, lining up the shades, then thread the needle.

4 Start stitching from the edges of the design, using long straight running stitches (see page 92) and voiding the areas between the double blue lines (see the instructions on page 22 for starting and finishing).

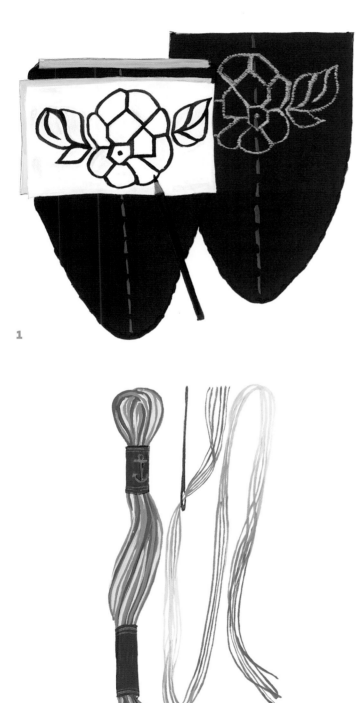

1

2

3

4

STARTING & FINISHING TECHNIQUES

1 To start, insert the needle in the middle of the motif leaving a ½" (12-mm) tail on top; make a tiny backstitch to secure, then start stitching from the extreme edge of design, so that the stitches cover the thread tail and hide it.

2 When the motif is completed, pull the thread through to the top of the fabric. Part the stitches and make a tiny backstitch to secure, pull tight, and cut—the thread tail should be hidden under the lines of stitches.

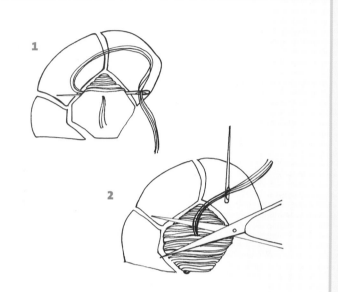

ALTERNATIVE COLORWAYS

Espadrilles always come in a wide variety of colors, and the embroidery can give different effects depending on the colors chosen. (This small motif could also be used to embellish other textiles, but because the stitches are quite long and vulnerable to catching, items that require folding are not really suitable.) Whether one, two, or four colors are used, the permutations are so varied that the same motif can look entirely different. Multicolored thread has been used throughout these alternative color schemes, but if solid colors are used, a more graphic effect is produced.

1 The colors in this embroidery blend with the ground fabric and with one another. There are no sharp contrasts between the mauve, blue, and bluish-green threads and the purple ground. The way to achieve this harmonious effect is to use adjacent colors from the rainbow for the threads and the ground— from purple to indigo blue to turquoise.

2 Just two different shaded threads have been used to stitch this vibrant embroidery. The effect is achieved by choosing flower colors that are opposite the ground color in the rainbow—here a bright pink on a green ground. The leaves and center have been stitched in the same lime green so that they stand out against the blue-green ground fabric.

3 Here the motif is stitched in another set of three complementary shades—red, orange-yellow, and green—but they have been placed on a contrasting bright blue ground so that they shine out.

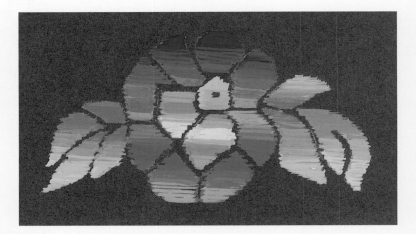

1

2

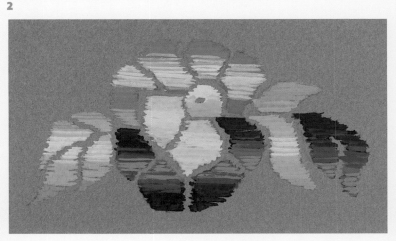

3

MULTICOLORED WOOL APPLIQUÉ

The design for this pillow was inspired by the appliquéd woolen penny or button rugs made in the mid-nineteenth century in America and Britain. Only tiny scraps of fabric were needed because the circles were traced around the circumference of various coins or other small circular objects. The original "pennies" were cut from men's wool suits or old blankets and each edged in blanket stitch to reduce fraying before being applied to a single piece of backing cloth with a central cross-stitch or star stitch.

In the design on the following pages, I have adapted the idea by embroidering three sizes of "pennies" together, using blanket stitch, in a bull's-eye pattern, so that the design resembles patchwork. The colors fall into two main groups: brights and neutrals.

If you wish, you can translate the design into other textiles by simply changing the backing fabric. For a pillow, calico is the best choice. For a throw, a matching or contrasting wool fabric would look good, backed with the original fabric that inspired the colors, perhaps. For a rug, a hard-wearing burlap or canvas backing is essential.

Bull's-eye pillow

The color scheme for this piece was inspired by a woven striped silk fabric. Because felt is available in such a large range of colors and can also be bought in small pieces, it is the ideal fabric for this design. I used a mixture of bright colors with a small selection of grays. For the soft cotton threads of the embroidery, I selected matching bright colors.

HOW TO MAKE THE PILLOW

Three sizes of "pennies" are together and then appliquéd onto squares of felt. The squares are applied in turn to a backing fabric, so that the design resembles patchwork. You will need to have sufficient bright and neutral colors to make good color contrasts; play with the color arrangements until you get a pleasing color balance. The appliqués are blanket-stitched onto each other, and the whole pillow is then finished with a blanket-stitched edging. The pillow measures 19" (48 cm) square. Once you have embroidered the pillow front, assemble the pillow as shown on page 103, and insert the pillow form.

MATERIALS

Felt pieces in 10 colors (five bright and five neutral), for 16 of
    each of the following sizes: ¾" (2-cm) circles ; 2¼" (6-cm)
    circles; 4" (10-cm) circles; and 4¾" (12-cm) squares
Two pieces of felt for pillow back, each 19" x 12¼" (48 x 31 cm)
Felt for pillow front, 19" (48 cm) square
Crewel embroidery needle, size 7
Pearl cotton size 8, one ball 80 m each in five bright colors
    (Anchor used for model)
Coats monofilament thread
Embroidery scissors and shears
Pillow form, 19" (48 cm) square

CREATING THE APPLIQUÉ

1 Using all four templates (see page 107), cut out sets of the three sizes of circle and the square, from each felt color.

2 Arrange the sets of circles and squares together so that the bright and neutral colors alternate. The following sequence of colors demonstrates a combination: a dark gray small circle on top of a lime medium-size circle on top of a pale gray large circle on top of a red square. Take some time to play with the colors to achieve pleasing combinations.

3 Start to embroider the sets together. First, stitch the small circle to the medium one with a star stitch (see page 98), using a contrasting *coton à broder* thread. Then stitch this, in turn, to the large circle with blanket stitch (see fig 2, page 95), using another contrasting *coton à broder* thread. Finally, stitch the large circle to the square, again using blanket stitch.

4 Arrange all the completed squares together on the backing fabric, with the neutral-colored squares and bright squares alternating. Pin and baste the squares in position so that no background shows. Then machine zigzag-stitch the squares to the backing fabric with invisible monofilament thread. Embroider over the seams with Cretan stitch (see fig 3, page 97), changing the thread colors to contrast with the different patches.

1

2

3

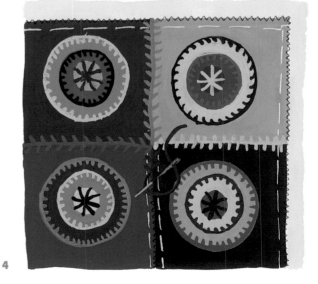

4

CHOOSING COLOR COMBINATIONS

It is possible to create many different looks using the same set of colors. For a completely different look, use just a few of the chosen colors from the range: all the brights or all the neutrals can predominate. The permutations are endless and, miraculously, the resulting embroideries will still blend with the original fabric that provided the inspiration for the color palette.

1 In this combination, all the neutrals have been used for the felt circles and squares, and the bright colors are confined to the embroidery threads. This has resulted in a muted and subtle embroidery that looks refined and lively at the same time. The felt pieces are still used to create an alternating light and dark design, placed on top of one another, then side by side so that each square contrasts clearly. The bright embroidery threads stand out clearly in a linear design against the softly toned ground.

2 This brilliantly colored design has omitted the neutral colors altogether, and the brights have been placed one against the other for maximum color contrasts and clashes—red against pink, backed onto lime green, lime against purple with spots of red and pink. The solid colors dance and vibrate when brilliant turquoise is used as a single color to embroider everything in position. It would look just as vibrant, and possibly even more dramatic, if one dark neutral was used for the embroidery. Using more than one color for the embroidery has an muting effect, because the eye is distracted by the varied stitch colors.

1

2

29

BEADED PATTERNS

In folk textiles all over the world, there is a long established tradition of decorating the existing patterns of woven and printed fabrics using embroidery or sequins and beads. In European embroideries the original pattern is sometimes completely covered, and certain Kashmiri shawls were woven with simple designs ready to be embroidered.

The advantage of this technique is that it requires less effort to create a strong impression, because the colors have already been selected and placed in position. As a result, it is an enjoyable introduction to stitching and beading. All you have to do is match the colors of the beads to the chosen print. Select a fabric that is basic in its details—blocks of color or simple well-defined shapes work best, because any subtle shading or linear drawing will be obliterated by the beads. Try not to cover the design completely or it will just look as if you have beaded onto a plain fabric.

On this evening bag, the beading is also enhanced with sequins and shisha mirrors. The beads are either strung on a thread and couched in position, known as lane or lazy stitch (see page 99), or stitched on one at a time, straight onto the fabric or through a sequin to secure it.

Beaded evening bag

This little bag has been beaded and embroidered using a mixture of beads, sequins, and shisha mirrors, following the pattern of the fabric. You can limit the extent of the beaded decoration, if you wish, to just a small section in the center of the bag. The fabric design used here is a simple, multicolored, irregularly spotted one.

HOW TO MAKE THE BAG

You will first need to enlarge and trace the bag shape (see page 106) and mark the area to be embroidered on the chosen fabric. Before you start the embroidery, you will need to strengthen the fabric to be embroidered with an iron-on interfacing. Once the embroidery has been completed, the bag is assembled as shown on page 101. The bag shown here measures about 8½" x 7½" (21 x 18 cm) and the handles are made from a pair of eyeglasses cords.

MATERIALS

Fabric with a circles pattern, 12" x 19½" (30 x 50 cm)—the fabric used here is Rowan "Bubbles" (see page 111)

Iron-on interfacing, cut to same size as patterned fabric

Selection of round beads, straight bugle beads, and sequins in different sizes, and shisha mirrors with embroidered surrounds

Medium-size transparent iridescent sequins

Short beading needle, size 12

Six-strand embroidery floss (to match the chosen beads, sequins, and shisha mirrors; Anchor used for model)

Water-soluble pen

Embroidery hoop or straight stretcher frame

Cords for handles and four small metal rings

Lining and lightweight fusible batting, each cut to same size as patterned top fabric

Embroidery scissors and shears

BEADING THE BAG

1 Iron the interfacing onto the wrong side of the patterned fabric, then fold it in half with the interfacing sides together. Using a water-soluble pen, draw the shape of the whole bag onto the right side (see page 106), aligning the base of the bag on the fabric fold line. Mount the fabric on a stretcher frame or hoop.

2 Use one strand of matching embroidery floss to attach the mirrors, sequins, and beads. First, slip stitch the shisha mirrors to the centers of the largest circles of color. Then sew the sequins to any other medium-size circles.

3 Surround the shishas and sequins and the remaining circles with the smaller beads, using different stitching patterns. Use the stitching patterns on page 34 or devise your own instead.

4 Scatter the transparent sequins onto the ground fabric. Secure each sequin to the fabric with a small bead at the center. To do this, insert the needle up through the central hole in the sequin, thread on the bead, and return the needle back through the central hole. The bead will keep the sequin in position. Assemble the bag as shown on page 101.

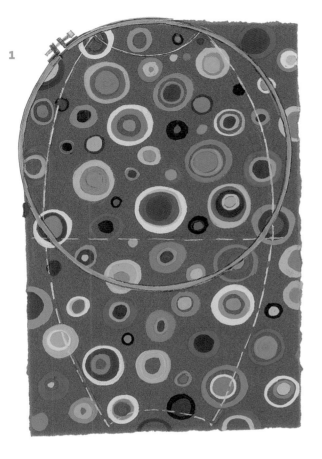

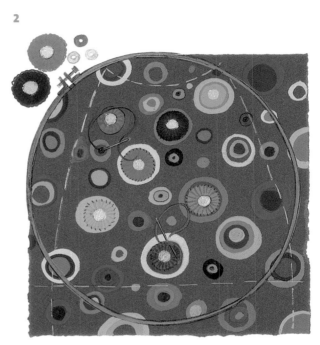

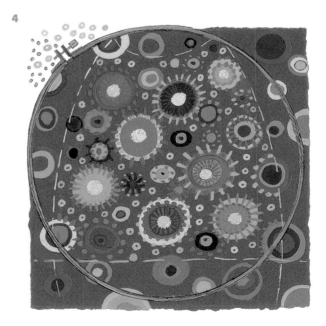

SHISHA VARIATIONS

Here are the different styles of stitching I have used for decorating the beaded bag. You can, of course, create your own designs if you prefer (see page 99 for lazy stitch).

Shisha mirror decorated with a row of medium-size round beads stitched to the edge of the shisha surround.

Shisha mirror decorated with large round beads placed at intervals around the embroidered surround.

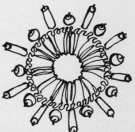

Shisha mirror with alternating bugle and round beads surrounding the embroidered edge.

Central sequin surrounded with small round beads; outer circle sequins secured with tiny beads and interspersed with small beads.

Small round beads stitched directly onto the shisha embroidered surround, with small sequins placed at the perimeter, each secured by a tiny bead.

Central sequin secured with a tiny bead, and a surround of alternating bugles and round beads.

Central sequin surrounded by tiny beads, with alternating spokes of bugles and rows of small beads.

Large central sequin secured with a small bead and decorated with spokes of rows of small round beads stitched on with lazy (lane) stitch.

Large sequin surrounded by spokes of large bugle beads.

BEADED DESIGNS

All types of patterned fabrics can be embellished with beads, sequins, or shisha mirrors. The main point to remember when selecting the decorative additions is to match the colors to the fabric. You do not have to create an allover pattern—the beaded decoration looks most effective when just a few areas of pattern have been embellished.

1 On a striped fabric, the central large stripe is embellished with shisha mirrors, with rows of bugle and round beads decorating adjoining stripes to create a glistening effect.

2 A regularly spotted fabric has been transformed with beaded and shisha decorations, the shisha and starburst bead designs alternating across the fabric in a repeating pattern.

3 A colorful floral fabric has rows of beads that simply follow the patterns of the stems with small decorative groups of beads to enhance the petals. The irregular patterns of the beads turn a basic repeat design into an exclusive "one-off" fabric.

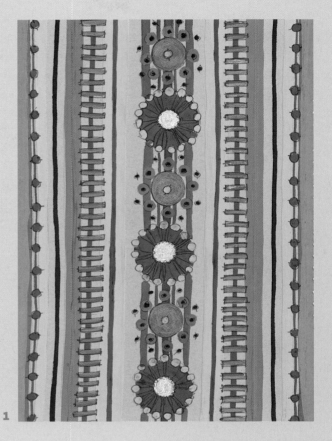

1

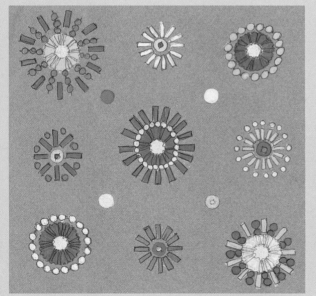

2

3

CRAZY PATCHWORK

Crazy patchwork is a form of appliqué that was extremely popular at the end of the nineteenth century in America and Europe. It is made from a myriad different patterned and plain fabrics overlapping one another in random patterns. The main decorative effect is achieved by embroidering the joins between each patch with different stitches in contrasting threads. In some of the richest pieces, the plain fabric patches are also embellished with embroidery.

The original crazy patchworks were often made from sumptuous fabrics, such as velvets, brocades, and silks, instead of the customary hard-wearing cottons and linens, but you can use whatever scraps of fabric you have at hand. For small items, like this book cover, you will need only a limited selection of fabrics. Limit the color palette to complementary colors for a harmonious effect.

Crazy patchwork book cover

This design, in complementary, differently patterned fabrics, is ideal for covering an album or a book, but you could very easily use the same concept for a picture frame (see pages 56–61), or even a pillow cover by enlarging the size of the patches. There is no need to copy the shape of the patches too slavishly, because you will be making up the patchwork from scraps of fabric. It is the random nature of crazy patchwork that gives it its charm, but it is probably best to use patches of roughly similar sizes.

HOW TO MAKE THE COVER

This crazy patchwork is worked by first arranging the patches on a backing fabric, then machine stitching them in place, and, finally, covering the raw edges with a decorative embroidery stitch. The secret to balancing the colors to create a harmonious design is to choose one or two strongly patterned fabrics and to select other plainer ones in colors that match those in the main fabrics. Make sure you have a wide selection of fabric colors so that you can choose at will. Instructions are given on page 105 for finishing the cover.

MATERIALS

Scraps of color-coordinated fabrics—the fabrics used here are
    predominantly Rowan patchwork cottons (see page 111)
Lightweight woven iron-on interfacing—for a large book cover,
    allow a piece at least 24" x 16" (61 x 41 cm)
Pearl cotton no. 5, in a range of plain and shaded colors similar
    to those in the chosen fabrics (Anchor used for model)
Crewel embroidery needle, size 5 or 6
Monofilament thread
Scissors
Water-soluble pen
Tape measure or ruler
Medium-size embroidery hoop
Sewing thead

CREATING THE PATCHWORK

1 Lay the book, opened flat, on the adhesive side of the iron-on interfacing. With a water-soluble pen, draw around the book, then add an extra 2" (5 cm) to the top and bottom of the rectangle, and at least 3" (8 cm) to the sides (for a wrap-around). Draw a line at the center to mark the spine position.

2 Select small pieces of fabrics and place the one with the strongest pattern on the backing fabric. Surround this with a few coordinating scraps, cut to overlap one another by about ¼" (5 mm). Using a warm iron, press the patches to the interfacing, protecting the adhesive on any uncovered areas with a sheet of paper.

3 Continue to assemble the patches in a pleasing pattern, filling in the whole surface of the interfacing and overlapping the outside edges a little. Press firmly in place (as in step 2). Then using invisible monofilament thread, machine zigzag-stitch around the edges of the patches.

4 Stretch the patchwork on an embroidery hoop and work over the seams, one at a time, with a decorative row of hand-embroidery stitches, using a contrasting-colored pearl cotton thread. The stitches can be various, but herringbone (see page 96), buttonhole (see page 95), and feather stitches (see page 97) are all traditional. Finally, lightly press with a warm iron.

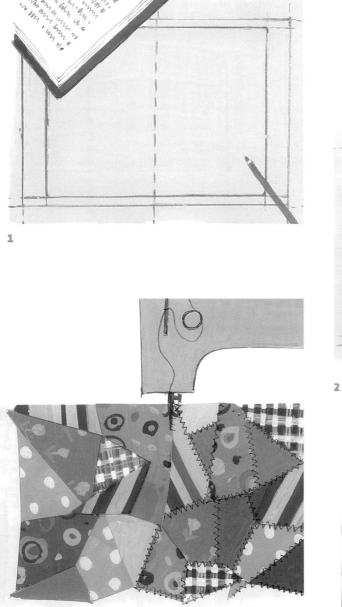

1

2

3

4

40

HEARTS APPLIQUÉ

Hearts, the universal symbol for love and affection, traditionally embellished children's covers and quilts, whether embroidered, woven, or patched. The reds used here, with vibrant pinks and richer shades of plum, symbolize the warmth and protective qualities inherent in this quilt designed for a crib or a small child's bed. The narrow strips of fabrics appliquéd with the embroidered hearts could be extended to make a larger quilt for a wonderful wedding gift. The fabrics are all traditional simple cotton prints and plains, embroidered with bold feather stitch in complementary red and pink pearl cotton. The quilt top, backing, and batting are "tied" together with knotted tassels of embroidery thread. Each heart is quilted separately with an outline of tiny running stitches.

Appliqué quilt

Narrow strips of patterned fabric, appliquéd with contrasting hearts in different patterns, make a simple design that works well on a small scale as a crib or baby quilt, or on a larger scale as a wedding quilt. Alternating strips of plain and patterned grounds give clarity to a very decorative design. The hearts, whether patterned or plain, have been placed on the ground that gives the strongest contrast. You could translate this design very successfully into a pillow, which would be quicker to make. Use just three rows of hearts for a rectangular pillow.

HOW TO MAKE THE QUILT

This baby quilt is made with three layers of fabrics—a quilt top, batting, and a backing fabric—which are tied together with knots of embroidery thread. The heart motifs are applied to the quilt top and stitched in position. The heart edges are embroidered with feather stitch (page 97). The embroidered top is worked first (shown right). Then the quilt is padded and tied, and each heart is quilted separately with an outline of tiny running stitches. The instructions for embroidering the top are given right. Instructions for assembling the quilt are given on page 44. This quilt measures 35" x 27" (90 x 68 cm).

MATERIALS

Five strips of different ground, three patterned and two plain, fabrics, each 28" x 8" (70 x 20 cm)
Cotton backing fabric, 36" x 28" (92 x 70 cm)
Batting, 36" x 28" (92 x 70 cm)
Mixed fabric scraps for heart motifs, patterned and plain
Embroidery scissors and shears
Fusible bonding web to back five strips of ground fabric
Monofilament thread
Embroidery hoop
Plain or multicolored pearl cotton no. 5 (Anchor used for model)
Crewel embroidery needle, size 5 or 6, and pins
Sewing thread

CREATING THE QUILT TOP

1 Enlarge and copy the heart motif from page 106. Back the fabric scraps for the heart motifs with fusible bonding web and cut out 15 hearts to the size required, using the heart template. Position three hearts across each strip of fabric. To acheive the maximum contrast, I suggest placing colored ones on a dark ground and patterned ones on a plain ground. Bond the hearts in place with an iron.

2 Secure the hearts by machine stitching around the edges using zigzag stitch and invisible monofilament thread.

3 Using an embroidery hoop to keep the fabric taut, hand embroider over all the heart outlines with feather stitch (see page 97), using contrasting shades of red and pink pearl cotton (space-dyed threads are ideal).

4 Arrange the strips of fabric, alternating plain with patterned ones. With the right sides together and using a ½" (1-cm) seam allowance, machine stitch the strips together. Press the seams open, then feather stitch over the seams with a complementary thread.

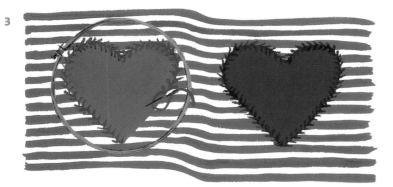

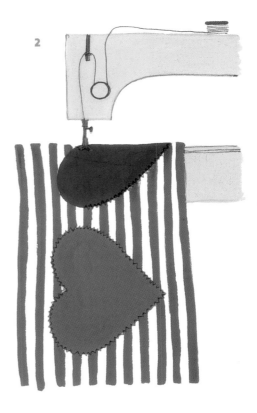

FINISHING THE QUILT

1 Pin the batting to the wrong side of the quilt top. Then pin the quilt top to the backing fabric with the right sides together. Using a ½" (1-cm) seam allowance, machine stitch around the edges, leaving a 6" (15-cm) gap at one side. Trim the seams and turn the quilt right side out through the gap. Close the gap with handstitches. Press lightly.

2 Pin the centers of the hearts, then handstitch a row of tiny running stitches around the outer edge of each heart using a matching sewing thread. Slip the stitches under the decorative feather stitched outline so the quilting is hidden.

3 Make a knotted tassel for each heart (see opposite), stitching them to the center of the heart through all the layers of fabric to secure.

1

2

3

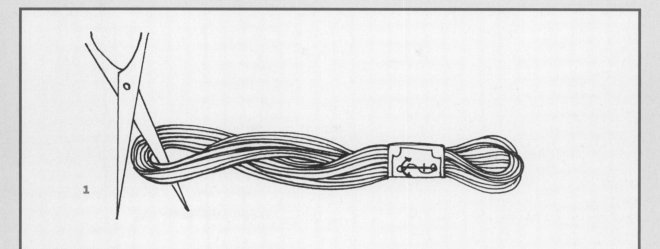

MAKING THE KNOTTED TASSELS

1 Cut four lengths of pearl cotton thread, about 1 yd (1 m) long, or use four strands from a cut skein of pearl cotton.

2 Fold three times and place in position. Thread the needle with a separate length of thread and stitch the strands firmly in place.

3 Tie a single knot around the stitching. Cut and trim the ends to the required length.

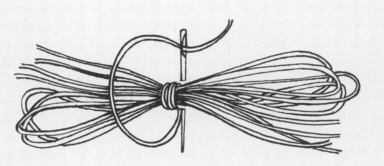

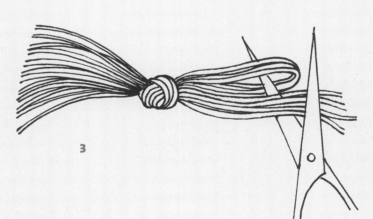

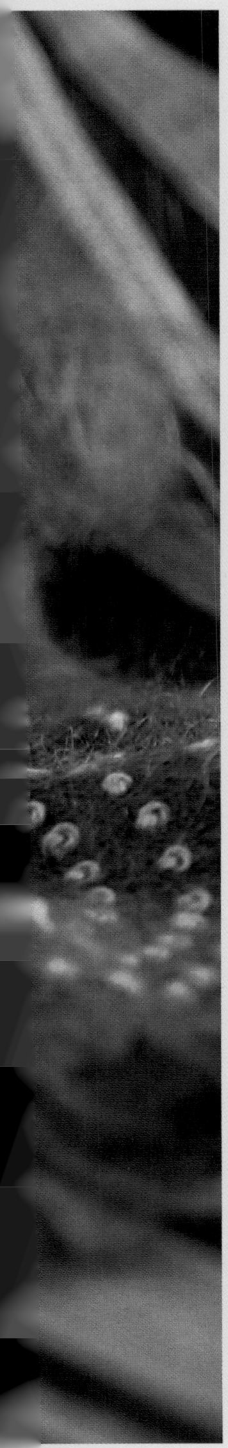

RAISED FRENCH KNOT DESIGNS

Small knots are a very useful textured and decorative stitch found in many countries under different names. In Chinese embroidery there is a decorative technique where entire motifs are stitched in clusters of knots using a slightly flatter version of French knots called Pekin knots.

Small round French knots are most often found in conjunction with candlewicking (see page 51) on early American bedspreads and they are usually white. The raised and precise knots act as a foil to sharpen and detail the more fluffy and softer areas of pattern formed by the candlewicking. However, used on their own French knots can describe intricate and curvaceous patterns, and they stand out well against brushed and piled fabrics.

The geometric nature of the little knots lends itself to abstract designs like the one shown here—based broadly on an ogee design, made popular in the Renaissance as a symbol for a flower bud—but you could use other simple geometric patterns for this kind of design.

French knot scarf

This fluffy mohair scarf has been given additional textural interest with a simple geometric pattern worked in French knots, positioned at each end of it. You could, if you prefer, use a plain wool as the ground fabric, but take care that the fabric is appropriate for knotting, which creates some tension on the threads. A similar design, perhaps in complementary colors, could be embroidered on a silk evening scarf.

HOW TO MAKE THE SCARF

This scarf measures 14" x 60" (36 x 150 cm). You can adapt the pattern to suit the width or size of the scarf (see page 88 for how to enlarge and reduce designs). This particular scarf is worked in wool tapestry yarn on a mohair ground, but if your scarf is a smooth, fine wool or silk, be sure to use an appropriate needle and thread. It is important that the knots sit on the surface of the fabric and do not pull through the weave.

MATERIALS

Wool scarf, either brushed or unbrushed

Four skeins of wool tapestry yarn, in a contrasting color (Anchor Tapisserie used for model)

Chenille needle, size 18

Water-soluble pen

Embroidery scissors

Tape measure

Straight stretcher frame

EMBROIDERING THE SCARF

1 Trace the design opposite and enlarge it so that it fits within the width of the scarf with at least 1½" (4 cm) to spare on each side. Redraw the line of the pattern on your enlargement in a strong color because you will need to see it clearly through the fabric when transferring it to the scarf. (Although this is not difficult if the fabric is loosely woven, if the chosen fabric is a solid wool, you will need to use the transferring method on page 88.)

2 Place the scarf on top of the design, which should be positioned so that the base of the design is 1½" (4 cm) from the bottom edge of scarf. Using a water-soluble pen, draw the outline on the scarf fabric.

3 Stretch the scarf on a straight frame. Then using wool tapestry yarn, start to stitch French knots (see page 94) along the pattern line. Follow the contours of the design exactly so that the stitching on the back forms neat lines—this way the design shapes will look the same back and front.

4 It may help to use a tape measure when stitching the first few rows of stitches because the knots need to be uniformly spaced, about ½" (1 cm) apart. As you get used to the rhythm of the stitch, or if you are already an experienced embroiderer, you can dispense with the tape measure.

1

2

3

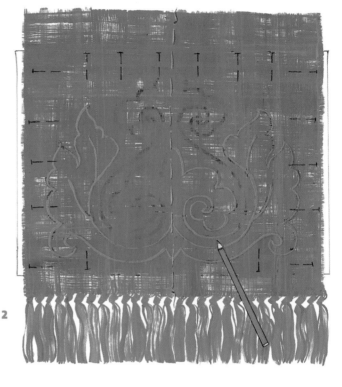

4

49

CANDLEWICK

Traditional candlewick decoration was worked on unbleached calico using a cotton yarn that is similar in appearance and thickness to the wick at the center of a candle, hence the name. The original designs, which involved looped stitches that were then cut to create a raised pile, incorporated many different patterns and stitches, and were used for beautiful bedspreads and carpets. The technique relied on washing the finished piece to fluff out the pile: the fabric would shrink when washed, trapping the cut loops securely in the ground fabric.

Brightly colored candlewick designs look best when bold, and lines and spots are relatively easy to work. The simple stitches I used are worked with multiple strands of yarn that fluff up to at least three times their initial size after washing. However, if you use modern preshrunk fabrics, an iron-on fusible backing fabric will be needed behind the embroidered areas to prevent the loops from being pulled through.

The effect of the technique on a colored ground is to enrich and darken it slightly, so choose a lighter shade of thread when matching the threads to the background colors.

Candlewick bolster

I have created a large bolster, ideal for a garden sofa, with a striped fabric. The fabric stripes dictate the candlewicking colors and patterns. You could easily turn this design into a smaller bolster, or a rectangular pillow, if you wish.

HOW TO MAKE THE BOLSTER

The bolster here is made in three pieces—a center piece and two end pieces—and measures 10" (25 cm) in diameter and 36" (90 cm) long. After working the embroidery, you assemble the bolster and add the cords and tassels at each end (see page 104 for assembly instructions).

Estimate the threads needed for your bolster—a skein of Anchor Soft Embroidery Cotton makes a 18" (50-cm) line of tufting and a 2" (5-cm) spot takes about 1½ skeins. You will need a very large-eyed darning needle for this technique, because the eye must be big enough to enable four strands of thread to pass easily through the fabric. If the fabric has been preshrunk you will need two pieces of iron-on interfacing the same size as the embroidered area of the bolster.

MATERIALS

2 yd (1.8 m) of striped fabric, 44" (112 cm) wide
Soft embroidery cotton in colors to match the stripes (Anchor was used for model)
Chenille darning needle, size 18
Water-soluble pen
Embroidery scissors and shears
Embroidery hoop or large straight stretcher frame
Iron-on interfacing, for backing embroidered areas
Soft embroidery cotton in suitable color for cords and tassels (Anchor was used for model)
Bolster to fit

EMBROIDERING THE BOLSTER

1 Mark the lines of stripes and spots at each end of the large central piece of fabric (see page 104). Draw the lines on each side of the spots so that they are different colors and use all the colors in the stripes.

2 Stretch the fabric on a hoop or straight frame. The tufted stitches are worked with two strands of soft embroidery cotton threaded in the needle, with the four ends aligned. Work the spots first, stitching small spirals in spaced-apart backstitch (see page 98), leaving a loop about ¾" (2 cm) long on the surface of the embroidery as you make each stitch. Using the needle, pull the loops away from the fabric often as you work to ensure that they are even in length. Cut all the loops in one spot before moving to the next one.

3 Work the tufted stripes on a stretcher or, if the hoop won't go over the worked spots, embroider them while holding the fabric in your hands—they are fairly quick and easy to work. Work the tufting as for the spots, but this time make the spaced-apart backstitches in a straight line. Cut through all the loops as you finish each line. When you have completed the four rows of stripes and one row of spots at one end, work the other end of the bolster in the same way.

4 Iron the pieces of interfacing onto the back of the embroidered areas and wash the fabric in hot water. Once it is dry and the cut loops have fluffed up, trim them carefully to an even height using embroidery scissors. Then finish the bolster (see page 104) and add the drawstring and tassels (see pages 54 and 55).

1

2

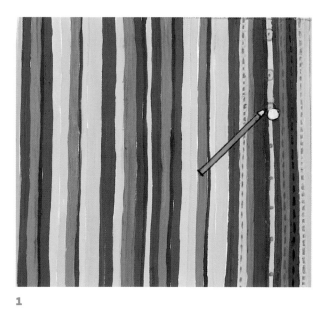

3

4

MAKING A CORD

The instructions here are for a two-toned cord.

You will need about 3 yd (2.5 m) of soft embroidery cotton in two colors to make the bolster cords, because the threads should be at least two and a half times longer than the required length of the finished cord. You will need a hook fixed securely into a board (or alternatively use a window catch or door handle, or anything that is solidly fixed).

1 Tie the first thread into a loop and place it over a hook. Place a pencil in one end of the loop and, keeping the threads taut, twist them clockwise until they form a tightly twisted cord—the longer the thread, the more twists required. This cord needs to remain taut and secured (fig. 2).

2 Twist the second thread exactly the same number of times in clockwise direction.

3 Place the two (or more) threads together, then twist them together in the counterclockwise direction, at least 15 times. When the thread starts to twist in on itself it is tight enough. Secure and cut off the knotted ends.

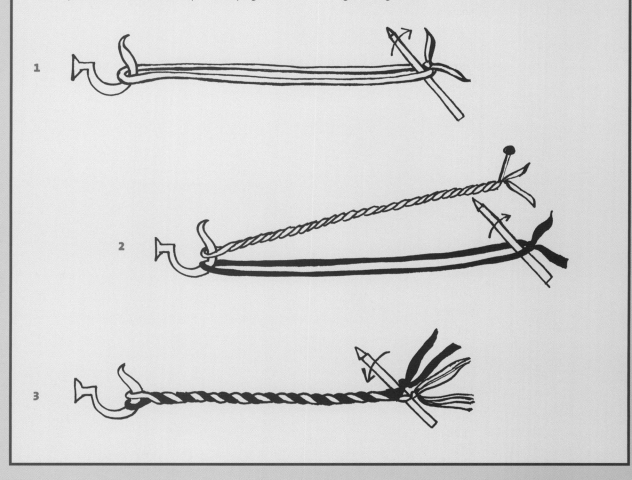

MAKING BOLSTER TASSELS

Tassels are an attractive form of decoration. An easy way to make a tassel, if it is wool, *coton à broder,* or embroidery floss, is to use the whole skein. If it is pearl cotton, you will need to remove the bands and fold the skein in half before proceeding as follows:

1 Remove the lower band and cut through all the threads at that end of the skein.

2 Tie the loops at the tops of the threads together to secure the tassel. Cut a long length of matching thread and make a loop in one end as shown, leaving a length of thread longer than the finished tassel.

3 Whip the other end around the top of the threads to form a neat spiral covering. To secure the loop, thread the end of the whipping thread through the loop and pull it so that the loop disappears under the whipping.

4 Thread the top end of the whipping yarn in a large needle and feed this into the center of the tassel. Trim the ends to level them.

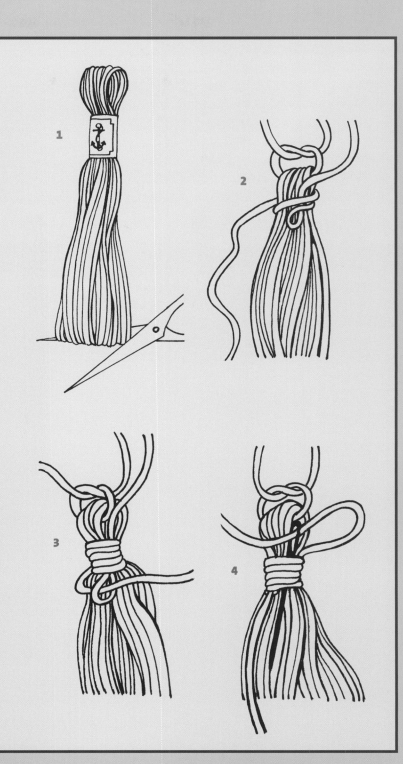

RUNNING-STITCH EMBROIDERY

Running stitch is the simplest and probably oldest stitch of all. Used as both a regular sewing stitch for basting fabrics together (before hand- or machine stitching), it also is one of the most popular embroidery stitches. It is the basic stitch for quilting fabrics together in a variety of designs and motifs, and it is also used for decorative darning, where it forms patterns of zigzags, diamonds, or crosses with rows of carefully worked counted-thread stitching.

The embroideries on the left are counted-thread designs, worked in straight lines of perfectly uniform and evenly spaced stitches. The key to this accurate spacing is the fabric that it is stitched onto: Aida is an evenweave fabric made specially for counted-thread embroidery, particularly for cross-stitch. Designed to be seen rather than completely covered like evenweave needlepoint canvas, Aida comes in a wide range of colors. It is available in different counts—11, 14, 16, and 18 stitches to an inch. Used here for picture frames, the fabric ensures that the stitches will be perfectly spaced in a smart and graphic pattern.

Running-stitch frames

Simple graphic embroidery designs and stitches are ideally suited to picture frames, as their linear quality does not distract the eye from the central image. It is a good idea when choosing colorways for the frame to use the color or style of the central image to direct your choice. In these two little frames, I have chosen a black ground with contrasting, brightly colored stitches for the black-and-white picture of the dog, and a bright red ground with complementary colors for the little flower picture.

HOW TO MAKE THE FRAME

You will need to either use a frame kit or make your own little cardboard frame, over which the fabric for the embroidery is stretched. Aida fabric is ideal for the ground fabric, because you can use the evenweave threads to ensure stitches of an even length. Using a separate needle for each color saves time because you do not have to rethread the needle for each new color. The running stitches used are shown on page 92. Once you have completed the embroidery, you will need to assemble the picture frame itself (see page 102).

MATERIALS

Cardboard frame kit or a piece of cardboard cut to correct
    format and size
Piece of 11-count Aida fabric in desired color, 2½" (5 cm) larger
    all around than the chosen frame
One skein each of soft embroidery cotton in at least seven
    colors—the dog frame, for example, uses Anchor red (46),
    pink (27), purple (98), blue (131), green (241), yellow (295), and
    orange (303); see page 60 for the flower frame colors
Batting, cut to same size as frame
Fabric glue
Tapestry needles, size 18 or 20
Embroidery scissors and shears
Silver fabric-marking pencil

EMBROIDERING THE DESIGN

1 Choose thread colors that complement or match the image you are proposing to frame, and that will contrast well with the chosen ground fabric (see page 60).

2 Lay the cardboard frame face down on the Aida fabric. Then draw around the outer and inner edges using the silver fabric-marking pencil—draw along the lines of holes to get an even line. Draw a line from each corner of the inner rectangle to create a brick pattern. Make sure that the same number of holes is counted for each section of the frame, to ensure even stitching over the whole frame.

3 Start stitching at the beginning of one of the four sections, using the first color and making a small backstitch outside the frame edge to secure. Stitch over three threads of ground fabric, under one thread, and over three threads to create the pattern. At the end of the row fasten off with another backstitch. Use the second color for the next row, placing it next to the first and leaving one set of threads unworked in between. Continue in this way with all the colors to complete the first side.

4 Start the next side of the frame, skipping one set of threads and working the first row in red. Repeat the colors (as for the first side) to the end of this side of the frame. Continue to space all the rows identically (with such a uniform design any mistake will be all too obvious when seen it from a distance).

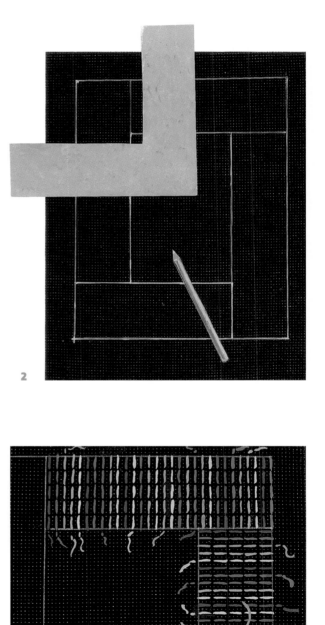

1

2

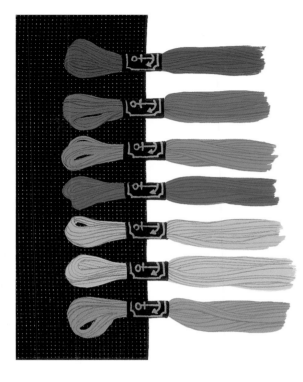

3

4

DESIGNING FRAME EMBROIDERIES

If you color-match the frame to the picture that it surrounds, even a detail of a postcard will look really special. If you make the frame quite a bit larger than the picture, the central image gains importance. For a square picture, cut a small square paper frame and place it over the area of the picture that you wish to frame. Tape this in position at the back and take it with you when you select the fabric and thread colors. First, decide on the color of the Aida ground, which will be the dominant color of the frame. Match the threads to the other colors in the central image by holding them close to it. Look really carefully at the colors because they are often different than what you would expect—the star shape in the image below looks white, but when you compare it with a white thread, it is, in fact, a creamy peach color; white would stand out too strongly if placed in the rows of stitches.

For the frame below, I chose two pinks to match the flowers, two purples for the vase, two greens—one soft and one brighter—for the leaves and stalks, and two blues from the centers of the flowers. Set all the threads against the picture with the ground color, and reject or replace any colors that jump out. In the frame opposite, a simple set of contrasting colors was used (see page 58).

The stitching instructions on page 58 can be adapted to suit any frame shape and size. For example, a smaller frame might need smaller, more closely spaced stitches.

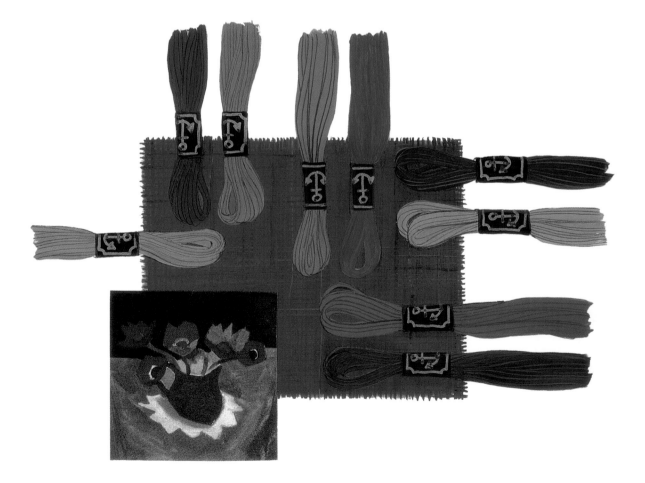

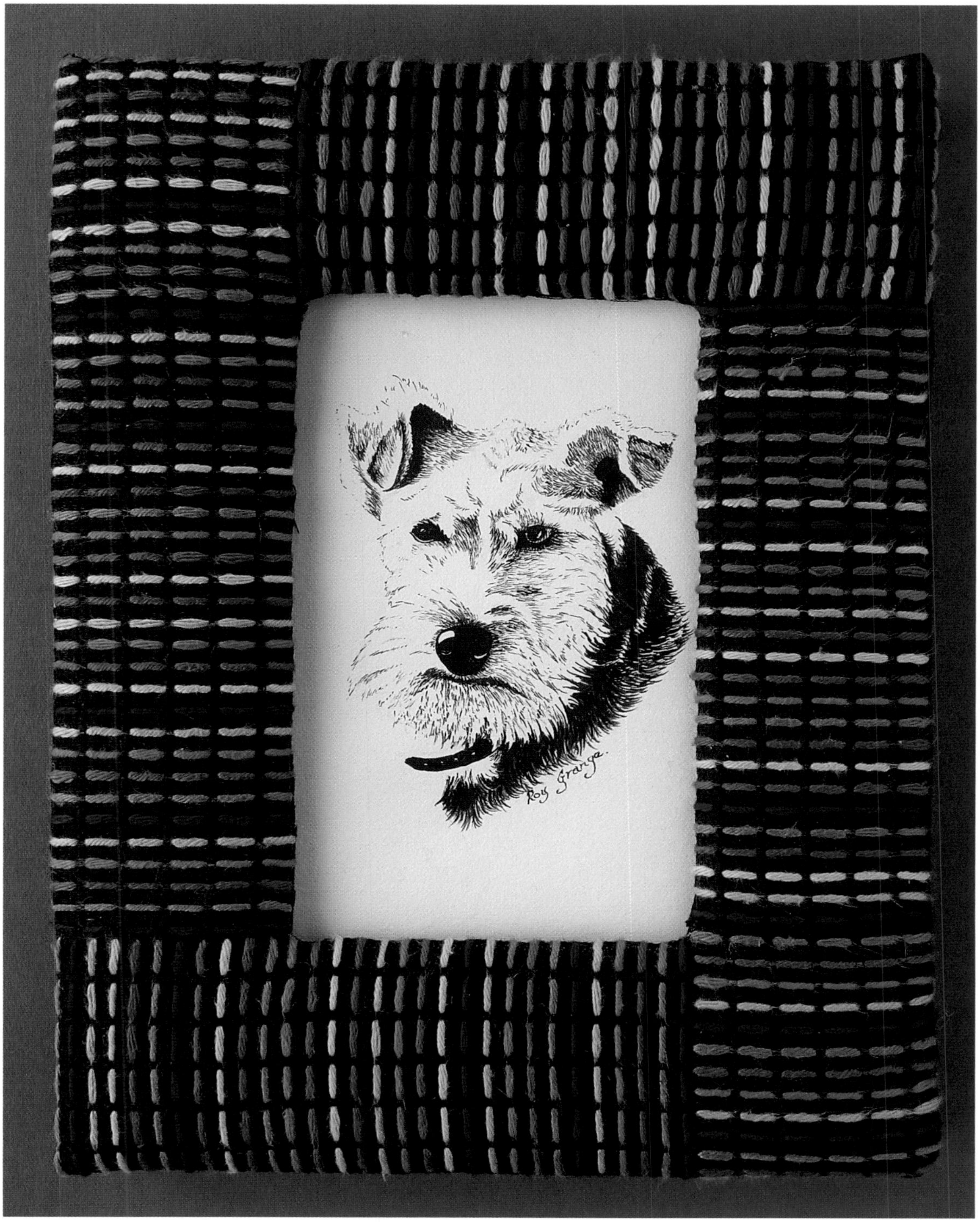

PICTORIAL MOTIFS

This rose and bow motif was inspired by the embroidered household linen so popular throughout Europe and American in the nineteenth and early twentieth century. Most girls were taught to stitch at an early age, and these motifs can also be found on European samplers of the same era, but on a much smaller scale.

In Germany and Switzerland particularly, romantic pictures of flowers, garlands, bows, and birds were stitched in fine linear designs on pillow covers, tray cloths, and pillows, and on bags used to carry home the freshly baked bread from the local baker. All kinds of images adorn this style of embroidery, including children dressed in costumes, complete with clogs and neckerchiefs, set against windmills. Household objects are employed, such as tea and coffee cups and pots—even sewing machines are depicted! The original embroideries were stitched in red or blue on white linen and are very elegant and crisp in appearance. The simple embroidered line used for the drawing is always subtle in its undulations: stem stitch is often used for the linear elements and satin stitch for the larger areas, to create an expressive and rhythmical motif.

Traditional floral motif

Here a favorite linen shirt has been given a new lease of life with a bright and contrasting-colored embroidery that decorates the pocket area. You could use the motif on a shirt or blouse, a bathrobe or kimono, or even on the pocket of a pair of jeans.

HOW TO MAKE THE MOTIF

You will need to first enlarge the motif on page 108, then transfer the design onto the chosen garment. It pays to pick out brightly contrasting colors when embroidering vividly colored garments, but a complementary motif can look good on deep-colored fabrics—for example on a pair of jeans. If you are embroidering onto or over a pocket, slip a piece of cardboard into it first, to make sure you do not stitch through the layers of the fabric. Before stitching fine fabric, to ensure it does not buckle, you should apply an iron-on interfacing to the back of the embroidery ground and stretch the area to be worked in a small hoop.

MATERIALS

Colored linen or cotton garment, with or without a pocket

One skein each of pearl cotton no. 5 in variegated red, variegated pink, lime green, and turquoise (Anchor used in model)

Medium-size embroidery hoop

Crewel embroidery needle, size 5 or 6

Iron-on interfacing, slightly larger than the motif

Dressmaker's carbon paper

Water-soluble pen

Embroidery scissors

EMBROIDERING THE DESIGN

1 Trace the motif from page 108 and enlarge it to the size required. Press the interfacing onto the back of the shirt front. Lay the shirt on a flat surface and place a piece of dressmaker's carbon paper over the area to be embroidered. Lay the motif design on top and, pressing very hard, transfer the design onto the fabric, drawing over any pocket as well.

2 Reinforce the drawing using a water-soluble pen, and if there is a pocket, draw a little extra stem inside it so that the pattern will be continuous even when the pocket gapes.

3 Place the hoop over the bow and stem section of the design, and if this is on top of the pocket, place a piece of cardboard inside it before starting to stitch. Thread the needle with the pink thread and stitch one whole bow outline in stem and satin stitch (see page 94), then fill the rest of the outline with the red thread using satin stitch. Next, stitch the stem (one side in lime and one side in turquoise), carefully finishing off the thread inside the pocket by running it inside the hem fold.

4 Move the hoop to the top section of the design and embroider the rose, the inside swirl, and enfolding petal in red and the outside petals in pink, using stem and satin stitch. Stitch the leaves with a mixture of green and turquoise thread, using the illustration, right, as a guide. Finally, stitch the stem, extending the stitching into the pocket if needed. Sponge off the pen marks and press with a steam iron on the wrong side.

ALTERNATIVE DESIGN COLORWAYS

These three alternative rose embroideries are worked with the same color principle as the shirt—that of working the motif in colors that contrast with the background. The theory behind this is shown in the introduction on pages 8 and 9 where the threads have been spread out to form a circular rainbow or color wheel. Opposite colors on the wheel contrast, so you will see that red and green are contrasts, as are orange and blue, or yellow and violet. When these color combinations are used together, the effect is always strong and bright, and sometimes so dazzling that the colors appear to vibrate. If, however, you want a softer and more relaxed look for your embroidery, work these colors on a complementary ground, picking a color nearest to it on the color wheel. For example, the reds and pinks could be embroidered on a soft mauve ground or the golden yellows and oranges embroidered on a cream ground.

On a blue ground the rose motif is embroidered in contrasting colors of golden yellow and orange, with the leaves worked in two shades of green. The warm tones of these colors look fresh and vibrant against the rich deep-blue ground fabric. The colors in this motif would look even more brilliant on a bright turquoise ground.

In this combination the violet and purples of the flower and bow are worked on a bright orange-yellow ground fabric. Can you believe that the green used for the leaves in this colorway is exactly the same color as the one in the other two alternative designs? From this, you can see just how colors behave when placed on contrasting colored, as opposed to complementary colored, grounds.

This hot magenta ground fabric has a lime green and citrus yellow embroidery as its contrast, while the same greens as before—a bluish-green and sap green—are used for the leaves and stalks.

FLAME-STITCH CANVASWORK

Flame stitch, Florentine, or Bargello are the popular names for this type of straight-stitched canvas embroidery. Variations of this technique, which rely purely on color for their effect, are found throughout Europe and America. It is most commonly used for covering household articles, because it is extremely hard-wearing. Chair seats, pillow covers, firescreens, and even rugs have been worked using this distinctive pattern. It normally relies for its effect on using tones of quite subtle colors, but I have broken with tradition by using different fresh and bright colors that all have similar tonal values and repeating the whole sequence of the design over the entire canvas, rather than opting for a small, repetitive pattern.

The technique is very simple and relies on counting either the threads or holes of the background canvas to ensure a perfectly patterned result. Each straight stitch is made over several threads—in this case over seven at a time. I chose the largest number advisable for the canvas count and the thickness of the wool, to make it as quick to stitch as possible.

Flame-stitch pillow

This small rectangular pillow would look good as the centerpiece of a collection of pillows in complementary colors. However, if you wanted to turn the design into a stool cover, for example, it would be possible to extend the design both horizontally and vertically to fit any rectangular shape. Because the pattern is worked over seven threads of medium-gauge needlepoint canvas, it is relatively quick to work.

HOW TO MAKE THE PILLOW

This pillow is easy to work. It measures 16" x 11" (40 x 28 cm) when finished. One color at a time is stitched across the whole canvas and each subsequent color is placed in exactly the same formation above and below it, creating a wavelike effect across the canvas. The chart for the pillow is on page 108 and shows a single line of color only. You will need a piece of canvas about ¾" (2 cm) larger all around than the proposed pillow. Once the embroidery is completed, assemble the pillow as shown on page 103.

Finally, make four tassels (see page 55) out of four different colors. Stitch each one to a corner using a matching thread.

MATERIALS

Piece of 12-count needlepoint canvas, 17½" x 12½" (44 x 32 cm)

Two skeins each of wool tapestry yarn in 7 colors (Anchor orange [8140], purple [8588], pink [8524], green [8986], lime [9274], yellow [9284], and green-blue [8918] used in model)

One additional skein each of four of these colors for the tassels

Medium tapestry needle

Water-soluble pen

Embroidery scissors and shears

Masking tape

Two pieces of backing fabric, each 12¼" x 12½" (31 x 32 cm)

Sewing thread

Pillow form, 16" x 11" (40 x 28 cm)

EMBROIDERING THE PILLOW

1 Having cut the canvas to size, stick the masking tape over the raw edges of the canvas to protect your hands and wrists from getting scratched and to prevent the edges of the canvas from unraveling. Using a water-soluble pen, mark a right angle ¾" (2 cm) in from the lower left-hand corner as a guide for the edge of the design.

2 Turn to page 108 for the chart. Using the purple thread, start stitching the design at the bottom left-hand corner. Knots are not used in canvaswork, so insert the needle from the back through the canvas, leaving a tail of yarn at the back (the tail will be secured when it is trapped with the subsequent stitches). Count six threads and return the needle to the back through the next hole, so that each stitch covers seven canvas holes. Follow the chart all the way to the top right-hand corner—the length of the stitch never changes, only the placement. Refer to stitch diagram for stitch sequence. When the first line of color is completed to within ¾" (2cm) of the edge of the canvas, draw the rest of the outline around the canvas, ¾" (2 cm) from the edge.

3 Stitch the second color in the same way above the first.

4 Once the whole sequence of seven colors has been completed, start again with the first color. When the embroidery is completed, steam press lightly on the back—there should not be any warping of the canvas as the stitches are straight.

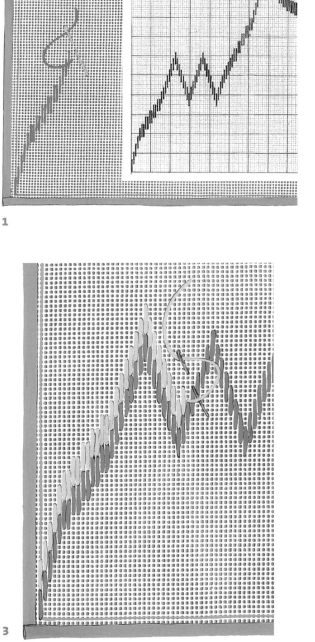

1

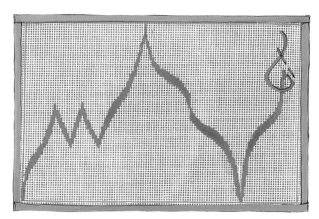

2

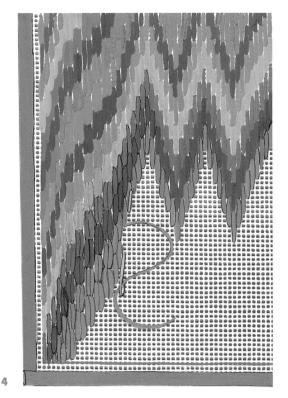

3

4

ALTERNATIVE DESIGNS AND COLORWAYS

In traditional Bargello patterns the colors are muted and follow one another in shaded variations. The colors I have chosen produce a strong and large allover pattern. There are many variations using the set of colors I have chosen here.

You will find that all the colors, except the lime, have both lighter and darker shades in the Anchor wool tapestry yarn range, and many different effects can be achieved by playing with the color placement. Sample several versions on a spare piece of canvas to get the look that you want. The resulting designs could be made into other projects in the book, such as the larger of the two bags (see page 76) or the book cover (see page 38).

1 In this example, the same set of colors are stitched in a more traditional system, with the colors following one another closely like a gradated rainbow. This causes the width of the zigzag to appear broader. Seen up close, it looks quite subtle, but when viewed from a distance it becomes a very strong pattern.

2 In this example, two colors have been chosen from the initial group—the pink and green—to which lighter and darker tones of the same color have been added to form a graduated striped zigzag effect.

3 In this example, all the colors have been used in a random pattern so that every potential color combination can be enjoyed. This would be a good starter for someone who just likes to use color, because they can stitch any they like together to form lively and contrasting patterns.

1

FELT FLOWERS

Felt is probably the oldest man-made fabric, consisting of layers of wool matted by water and heat into a continuous, solid sheet. As it is not woven, it does not fray when cut and this makes it very easy to use. Felt has been used as a basis for embroidered wool rugs in India and for appliquéd blankets in the Balkans. It has always been popular as a material on which children learn to stitch because it is so easy to cut and sew.

Felt is now mostly made from synthetic materials and is usually easily obtained in a wide range of bright colors. Modern felt-makers experiment by embedding different materials into the felt, but the design shown on these pages emphasizes the beauty of the matte finish, using a harmonious choice of colors.

The three-dimensional felt flowers depicted were very popular during the latter years of the nineteenth century and in the early twentieth century. They were usually wired up into small bunches to wear as a corsage or as single flowers to decorate a hat. Here a few flowerheads have been arranged above a basket shape on a pieced felt ground. The design could be used to decorate many different items, from a tea cozy or pillow cover to a book cover or a bag.

Felt-flower bag

This retro-style design has been used for a simple fabric shopping bag. You can make the design and apply it to a store-bought bag, or you can use the design for a pillow cover. The choice of complementary colors helps to pull the design together, but you can opt for a similar blend in, say, mauves, blues, grays, and pinks.

HOW TO MAKE THE BAG

You will need felt pieces in five complementary colors. The bag shown here measures 15" (37 cm) square, so the two main colors (turquoise and mauve) need to be cut to fit the width of the chosen bag. You can make the design on a piece of ground fabric and then simply sew it neatly to the chosen bag. To make a pillow, see page 103.

MATERIALS

Store-bought canvas bag

Turquoise felt, 16" x 8" (40 x 21 cm), for top background

Mauve felt, 16" x 5½" (40 x 15 cm), for bottom background

Small pieces of felt in light blue, pink, mauve, and lime green, for appliqué

½ yd (50 cm) of backing fabric

Two skeins each of soft embroidery cotton in pink and pale lime (Anchor used in model)

Crewel embroidery needle, size 18

Water-soluble pen

Embroidery scissors and shears

Pins

Sylko sewing thread

STITCHING THE EMBROIDERY

1 Place the pieces of turquoise and mauve felt on the backing fabric, and pin and baste in position. Using the pattern for the basket on page 107, cut out the basket shape from light blue felt and pin in position on the center of the background, aligning the seam allowances. Using soft embroidery cotton, embroider herringbone stitch (see page 96) between the two background colors and work Jacobean trellis stitch (see page 99) onto the basket, using the thread colors shown.

2 Using the patterns on page 107, cut out the leaves from lime green felt and small circles from light blue felt and assemble the three-dimensional flowers as shown on pages 78–79.

3 Arrange the flowers in position on the backing. Pin and baste a lime green circle of felt in the center of each flower, and work a star stitch (see page 98) in pale lime soft embroidery cotton to secure it.

4 On the round-petaled flowers, work a pink French knot (see page 94) in the center of each petal so that they won't droop too much when used. Catch the backs of the folded-petal flowers with a few stitches in a matching sewing thread. Position the small light blue dots of felt between the large flowers, and work star stitches in pink to secure them. Stitch the leaves in position with a pale lime soft embroidery cotton, using running stitch (see page 92).

1

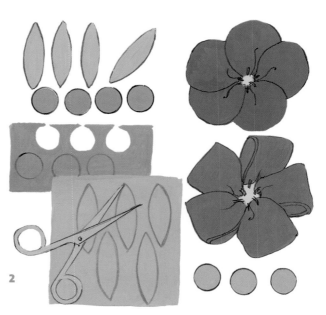

2

3

4

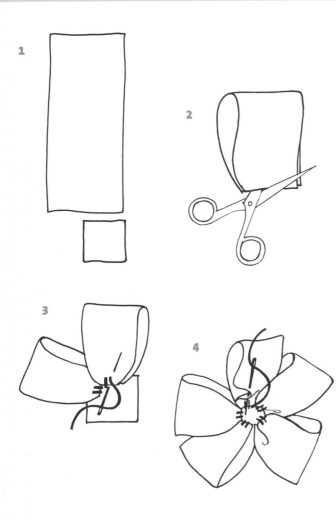

MAKING FOLDED-PETAL FLOWERS

1 Using the patterns on page 107, cut five pieces of mauve felt measuring 2⅝" x 1⅛" (7 x 3 cm) and one small ¾" (2-cm) mauve square. Cut one central disk ¾" (2 cm) in diameter from lime green felt.

2 Fold each rectangle of felt in half and trim the base corners for the petals.

3 Stitch the folded petals to the small square with a few straight stitches in a matching thread, overlapping the base edges of the petals.

4 Make a little tuck at the left-hand bottom edge of each petal so it folds softly over the next petal.

5 Place the flower on the background, position the central circle, and using pale lime soft embroidery cotton, stitch a star stitch (see page 98) through all the layers to secure.

MAKING ROUND-PETAL FLOWERS

1 Using the patterns on page 107, cut five petal shapes and a small square from mauve felt, and a central disk from lime green felt.

2 Make a small tuck in the center of the base of each petal and secure with a few straight stitches in a matching thread.

3 Sew the petals to the small square of felt, overlapping each one on the left-hand side. Finish as for step 5 of the folded-petal flower.

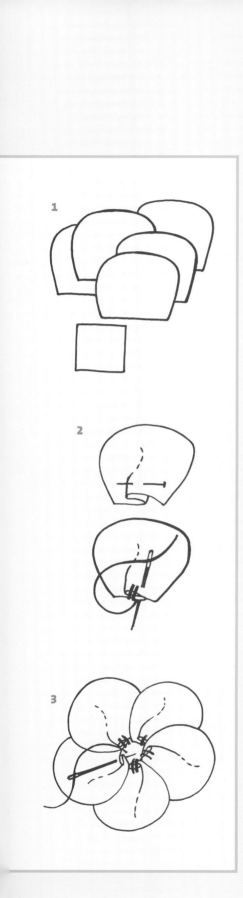

1

2

3

SHISHA MIRRORS

The shisha mirrors and sequins used in this little hat traditionally decorate children's hats and garments in southern India. Mirrors and shiny sequins are featured on many tribal embroideries because the sun glinting on the surface dazzles the eyes and this is thought to deflect the "evil eye" away from whoever is wearing the garment, so precious children are doubly protected by little hats like this one.

There are many ways in which the little pre-embroidered mirrors now available can be further embellished, and they are easily stitched into position with a few hidden slip stitches. Traditional Indian embroidery features many round stitching patterns for working in conjunction with the mirrors. These are always executed in brilliant colors, and sometimes tiny metal sequins that further reflect and refract the light are stitched between the mirrors.

I have designed a little hat and belt in this style, but you could choose to apply the mirrors, if you prefer, to a small round pillow or perhaps the cuff or hem of a garment.

Shisha-mirror hat

The design for this little hat is very simple to make—just a circle of fabric for the crown with another band of fabric stitched to it. If you prefer, you can make an even easier alternative—the decorated belt shown on page 85. The pre-embroidered mirrors and sequins come in a wide range of colors, but will look most attractive when the ground fabric tones and the mirrors are in the same tonal range.

HOW TO MAKE THE HAT

First, you will need to cut out the hat pieces from felt. You then embroider the crown and sides of the hat with the mirrors before stitching the hat pieces together. Follow the steps, right, to embroider the hat, then the finishing instructions on page 84 for stitching the hat pieces together. The diameter of the hat measures 7½" (19 cm). One size fits all as there is a small vent at the back.

MATERIALS

Mauve felt, about 12" x 24" (30 x 60 cm)

Light blue felt for lining, same size as mauve felt

Iron-on medium-weight interfacing fabric for hat band, 2½" x 22" (6 x 56 cm)

30 pre-embroidered shisha mirrors, in pale blue, peach, mauve, and lime green

Packet of silver sequins

Two skeins each of rayon embroidery floss (Anchor Marlitt in pale blue [1009], peach [1044], mauve [816], and lime [1029] were used in model)

One skein of rayon embroidery floss (Anchor Marlitt in lime green [1029], for stitching the borders used in model)

Embroidery needles, sizes 9, 7, and 3

Water-soluble pen

Embroidery hoop (optional)

Embroidery scissors and shears

EMBROIDERING THE HAT

1 Using the mauve felt, mark and cut the patterns pieces (see page 109) for the hat band and crown, leaving a good allowance around the edges if you want to use an embroidery hoop. (You may have to cut the hat band in sections if you are using small pieces of felt, so allow an additional ½"/1 cm for each seam.) With a water-soluble pen, mark the circles shown on the patterns.

2 Sew on the first mirror to the center of the crown with slip stitch, using one strand of matching Marlitt thread and size 9 needle. Using all six strands of thread and the size 3 needle, embroider the larger circle pattern using the pen line as a guide (see fig 5, page 97).

3 Pin the next circle of mirrors in position, using the other colors, and embroider them, alternating three large circle designs with three small ones (see fig 4, page 97). When completed, put in the last circle of mirrors, using all the colors and alternating the circle sizes as before. Place the sequins in any gaps between the embroidery, sewing them on using a French knot, three strands of lime thread, and the size 7 needle (see page 94).

4 Embroider the band of the hat in the same way, using all the colors and placing sequins in any gaps. Press lightly on the backs of the embroideries, using a warm iron. The hat pieces are now ready to be stitched together.

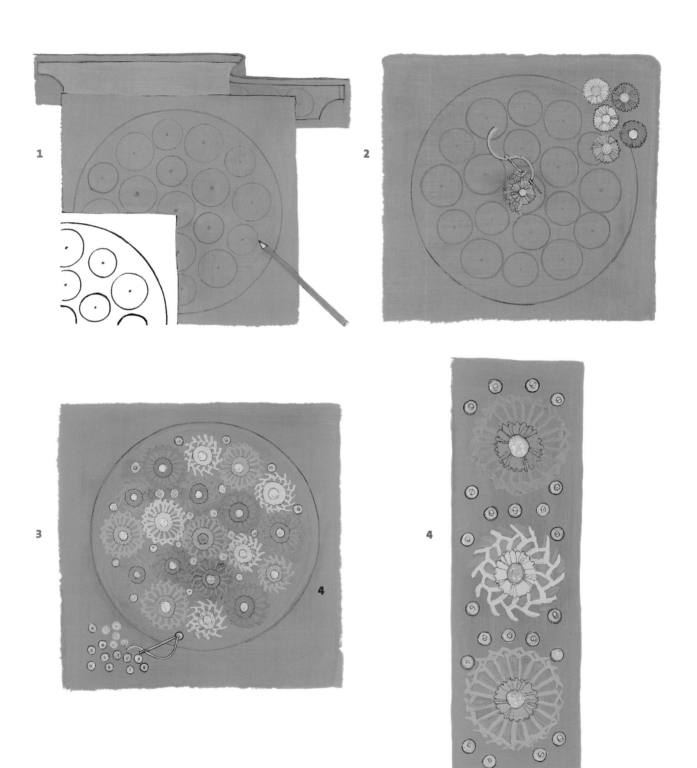

1

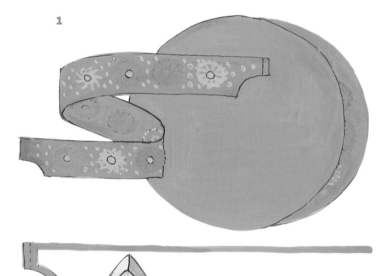

2

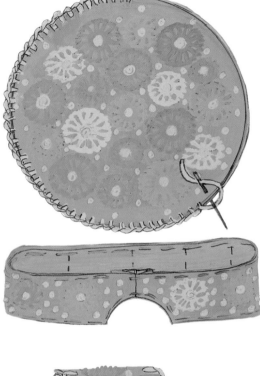

3

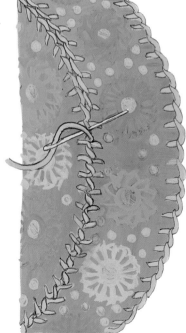

FINISHING THE HAT

1 Cut out the crown and the band to the correct sizes, and cut the felt linings and interfacing for the band to the same sizes. Iron the interfacing onto the inside of the hat band. Sew the ends of the band together and press the seam allowances back over the interfacing.

2 Sew the ends of the lining band together in the same way, then place the lining inside the embroidered band, with the wrong sides together. Pin and baste. Pin and baste the crowns together and work blanket stitch (see page 95) all around the outside, using all six strands of lime thread and the size 3 needle. Work blanket stitch around the band in the same way.

3 Place the crown and the band together and pin at intervals. Using 6 strands of lime thread, join the pieces by stitching together the two outside threads of the blanket stitches.

Shisa-mirror belt alternative

This bright belt consists of two bands of felt in contrasting colors, decorated with shisha mirrors stitched with contrasting colored threads, and tied with a shiny cord. Cut out two pieces of felt to the chosen length and width of the belt, and cut out a piece of iron-on interfacing to match.

1 Mark the positions of the mirrors along the length of one felt strip, about 2½" (6 cm) apart. Remove the centers from four of the mirrors and set aside the surrounds. Embroider the mirrors with contrasting threads, positioning one empty one at each end of the belt. Cut eyelet holes inside each empty surround. Cut off the corners at each end and iron the interfacing onto the back of the other felt strip.

2 With wrong sides facing, pin and baste the layers together. Work blanket stitch around all sides using a contrasting thread. Cut eyelet holes in the backing inside the empty surround at each end and stitch empty surrounds to the backs of the eyelets. Knot on two lengths of cord through the eyelet holes for the ties.

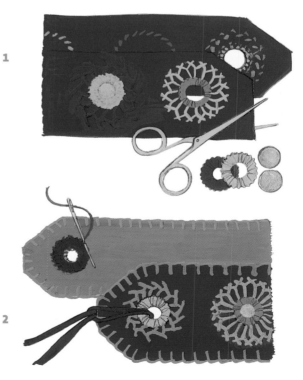

USEFUL
INFORMATION

Basic embroidery techniques

Most of the projects in this book are very straightforward. You will, however, have to acquire a few basic

design techniques, namely, resizing designs and transferring these to your embroidery fabric (the designs,

patterns and/or charts for some of the projects are given on pages 106–109). A few embroidery

techniques, primarily how to stretch the ground fabric, are also essential.

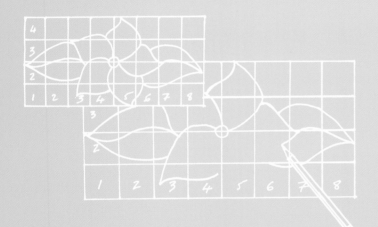

RESIZING DESIGNS

The most important decision to be made is the size of the design. Is it the correct size for your purpose? If not, the easiest way to change it is to use a photocopier either to reduce or enlarge it, but the traditional method for resizing is to redraw the design on a grid. Draw a grid over the initial tracing (using ½"/1-cm squares); this is the usual size for small motifs. Decide how much bigger or smaller to make the design. Then draw another grid on a separate sheet of paper using the same number of squares but resized to fit the chosen dimensions; here the squares have been enlarged by 50 percent. Transpose the drawing by matching the lines square by square.

TRANSFERRING DESIGNS

The next decision to make is the method to use to transfer the design to the ground fabric. The choice depends on the fabric and the type of design.

Light fabric method

If the fabric is transparent or very light in color, it is easy to lay the fabric over the tracing, secure it with pins, then draw over it using a water-soluble pen. If you tape the fabric to a light source, such as a window pane, you can see through slightly thicker fabrics.

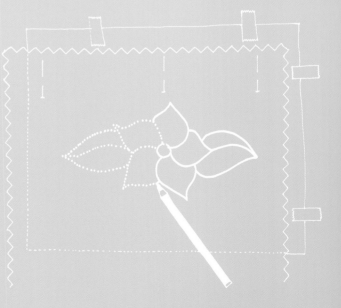

Carbon paper method

When the fabric is thick and opaque, the transferring system using dressmaker's carbon paper is the best one to opt for. Place the fabric on a hard surface and put a sheet of the carbon paper, color side down, on top of it. (Use a color that contrasts with the ground fabric but one that is not too dark or it may take a few washes to get rid of the mark.) Secure the tracing of the design in position, using a few pins, then trace over the lines with a ballpoint pen or a very sharp pencil.

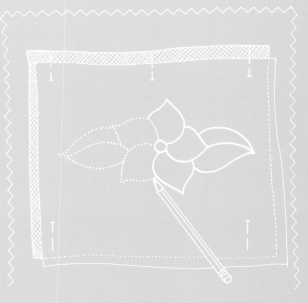

Transfer paper method

If the design is symmetrical (in other words, if the mirror image is identical to it), then you can use special transfer paper. All you have to do is to draw the design straight onto tracing paper using the special transfer paper (fig 1). Then turn over the paper and place the marked side next to the fabric, pin in position, and press with a cool iron (fig 2). The heat of the iron transfers the drawing onto the fabric, and the design is washed out when the embroidery is complete.

1

2

PREPARING TO STITCH

When stitching designs onto fine or soft fabrics it is advisable to stretch them before working on them, even if they are backed with another fabric for stability. Stretching ensures that the fabric lies flat after embroidery and does not pucker, shrink, or distort owing to the tension exerted by the constant pulling of the stitches through the fabric. The design must be transferred onto the fabric first by any of the methods on pages 88 and 89; then, depending on the size of the motif, either a round hoop or a rectangular stretcher frame is used.

Working with a hoop stretcher

Hoop stretchers come in a variety of sizes, from very tiny ones to large quilting hoops. They are made of two wooden rings, with a screw adjuster. To mount the fabric, slip it over the inner hoop, and lay the outer hoop over the fabric. Then stretch the fabric taut by adjusting the screws. Hoops are easy to use because you can slip off the work by just loosening the screw on the outer ring.

To ensure precise stitch placement, when working with the hoop stretch the fabric as tightly as possible without distorting the motif—it should ping when you flick it with your fingers. If you are right-handed, always work with the screw at the top left of the hoop (fig 1); if you are left-handed, it should be at the top right. This prevents the thread from catching on the tightening device.

It is advisable when stretching fine or slippery fabrics, satin or lightweight silks, to wrap the under ring with a length of soft muslin or fine cotton (fig 2). This protects the delicate fabrics from the harsh wooden surface and also ensures a tighter grip. If very delicate fabrics are used, you can also wrap the outer ring in the same manner, securing the ends with a few tacking stitches to prevent the cloth from unraveling.

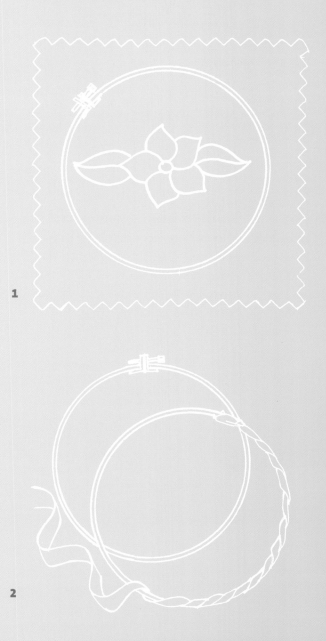

1

2

Working with a straight stretcher frame

A straight stretcher frame is useful for large items and fabrics that would mark if a hoop were used—velvet, for example, would mark and require steaming to correct, and the threads of very fine gauze would distort and be ruined if stretched on a round stretcher. Like the round frames, straight frames come in various sizes as big as 1 yd (1 m) in length. The most versatile straight frames are those whose horizontal bars are rollers, because the fabric can be rolled around the top and bottom bars so that only a small amount of the surface is exposed at one time.

Stretching fabric on a frame

First, pin then baste the ends of the fabric to the strips of fabric tape attached to the top and bottom bars of the frame. Apply tension by rolling the fabric so that the surface is evenly stretched top and bottom and the area to be embroidered is revealed. Ensure further tension by lacing the fabric to the vertical bars at each side (fig 1). These stitches will need to be removed when another section of the embroidery is to be rolled on to be worked, and the process then repeated. An extra strip of fabric can be basted over the base of the work to protect it from getting dirty (fig 2).

1

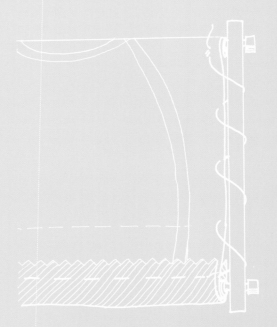

2

Stitch glossary

Learning to embroider is like any other skill: it requires a little practice to master it. But unlike many other crafts, embroidery is easy enough for a child, as you can see from the many excellent stitch samplers that children as young as seven or eight years old produced in days gone by.

I have concentrated on basic stitches in this book, with one or two special ones for specific purposes. As in any other crafts, keen embroiderers often create their own working methods, and there is nothing to prevent you from working the stitches in a way that suits you best. There is a great deal of satisfaction to be had in achieving sufficient manual dexterity and control to produce stitches of a similar weight and length, and it is just this regularity that will give your work its desired elegance and appeal.

The threads you use will make a great deal of difference to the effect produced by the stitches. For example, space-dyed yarns can be used to produce finely graded color effects. Choosing the right stitch and appropriate thread for the purpose is a key element in achieving a professional finish.

RUNNING STITCH

The simplest stitch in a group known as straight stitches, running stitch involves simply passing the needle and thread in and out of the fabric in a line. It can be used to outline a motif and is one of the most frequently used stitches in quilting. When used to solidly fill a motif it is called darning stitch.

If you are right-handed, running stitch is worked from right to left. You need to create a rhythm that allows you to weave the needle in and out easily and with regular spaces between the stitches. Normally, you take two to three stitches at a time on the needle before pulling the thread through, but on thick fabrics (for example when quilting) you may have to stab the needle through the layers of fabric, picking up only one stitch each time (this is known as stab stitch).

CROSS-STITCH

Also known also as sampler stitch or Berlin stitch, cross-stitch is internationally popular and is found on traditional embroideries in countries as far apart as Greece, Scandinavia, and India. A geometric stitch in the straight stitch family, it is worked on evenweave fabric, which enables you to produce perfectly even stitches by counting threads. Using waste canvas allows you to create even cross-stitches on other fabrics. There are many variations of this stitch, but basic cross-stitch is both effective and popular.

Cross-stitch patterning can be achieved by working the stitches in rows. When shaped areas of design are to be covered, such as a letter, it is advisable to work the stitches in rows and count each row as you go. This method helps to achieve the correct positioning of the top arm of each crossed stitch, so that it faces in the same direction as all the others in the embroidery, which adds greatly to the harmony of the finished work.

BACKSTITCH

One of a group of straight stitches, it creates a line of stitches with no space between them, looking rather like a drawn line. To create similarly sized, even backstitches requires a little practice, so try out the stitch, both on straight lines and curves, to perfect your technique. The stitches are worked so that the needle is taken back to the finishing point of the first stitch, to create an apparently continuous line.
(Note: In the tufting variation used in the candlewick technique, the backstitches are spaced slightly apart and long loose loops are left on the right side to form the tufts.)

SPLIT STITCH

Looking like a tiny chain stitch, split stitch is a variation of backstitch, because it is worked in the same manner, except that the needle goes through the preceding stitch.

SATIN STITCH

One of the most widely used stitches in embroidery, satin stitch is used most frequently as a filling stitch. Made up of straight stitches worked close together in parallel lines, it is particularly useful for monograms, where it is padded to raise the stitch from the ground fabric and give the motif a three-dimensional effect. The length of the stitches varies—short stitches at the point of a leaf and wider stitches toward the base—but very long stitches need to be avoided as they look untidy and can snag. Normally, when filling a motif you make the shortest stitches first, working in parallel lines. To ensure an even outline, it pays to work the outline first in backstitch.

In order to create really even stitches, you will need to stretch the ground fabric in an embroidery hoop or frame.

STEM STITCH

This linear form of satin stitch, known as stem stitch, is worked as a series of short, straight stitches placed close to one another to form a continuous line.

FRENCH KNOT

These little jewel-like stitches are created by winding the thread around the needle in the course of making the stitch, so that each stitch resembles a small bead. They are useful for creating textural effects. An embroidery hoop is useful for keeping the ground fabric taut. Practice will help you create neat, even knots.

BULLION KNOT

For this elongated version of the French knot, use a firm thread and a milliner's/straw needle so that the thread can pass easily through the coils, which must not be allowed to slip out of place as they are pulled into the reverse position to anchor the stitch.

BUTTONHOLE AND BLANKET STITCHES

One of the most popular and most useful of looped stitches, buttonhole stitch (fig 1) and its close cousin, blanket stitch (fig 2), are worked in exactly the same way, but in buttonhole stitch, the stitches are placed close together to form a single line of stitches, whereas in blanket stitch they are positioned a short distance apart. Both stitches are used to finish off raw edges and prevent them from fraying. As with all embroidery stitches, even, neat stitches are essential for a professional finish. To stitch a corner in blanket stitch, it is advisable to work an extra stitch on a slant into the corner as shown (fig 2).

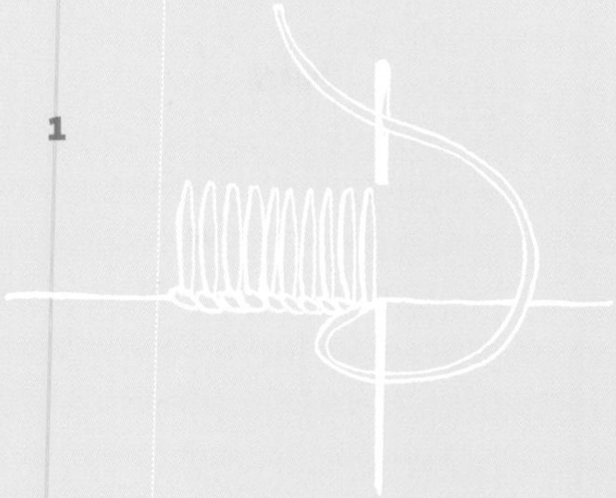

DECORATIVE BLANKET STITCHES

Decorative versions of blanket stitch are useful for edging pillows and throws. A closed blanket stitch variation (fig 3) forms neat triangles and gives a very crisp finish. A circular blanket stitch variation (fig 4) is useful for florets and in traditional smocking embroidery.

DETACHED CHAIN STITCH

Chain stitch is a looped stitch (known as tambour stitch in the East where it is worked with a fine hook). It is used primarily as an outline stitch but can also be worked close together in fine thread to make filling stitches. In the variation shown here (known as detached chain or lazy daisy stitch) the thread is looped under the point of the needle to make an extra small straight stitch, before the needle is inserted back into the ground fabric to create the next chain stitch.

1

2

3

4

HERRINGBONE STITCH

A traditional stitch in the cross-stitch family, herringbone stitch comes with many pseudonyms, as it is practiced in many parts of the world. The slanting, crossed stitches are useful for joining fabrics together and prevent edges from fraying. They can be worked in many different ways to subtly alter the formation, so that in some versions the top of the row of herringbone stitches is more widely spaced to create a lattice effect. Its geometric look demands precision, so practice first to ensure your stitches are evenly worked.

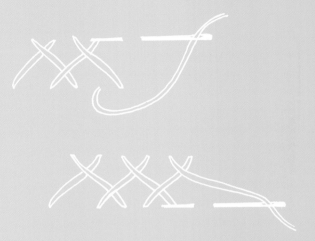

Variations

There are many stitches that can be added to the crossed sections of herringbone stitch to produce some highly decorative and very elegant lines of embroidery.

The extra stitches can be worked in threads that contrast with the base of herringbone stitches.

1 Running stitches are placed over the two sets of crossed stitches. One line is sewn at a time.

2 Straight stitches are sewn vertically over the crosses. These can be stitched in a single row at a time by alternating between the upper and lower stitches.

3 The combination of theses two stitches, running and straight, makes a cross-stitch variation.

4 Single chain stitches decorate the herringbone line. These can be repeated on the upper line of crosses for a very decorative effect.

1

3

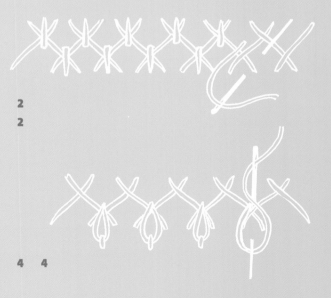

2
2

4 4

FEATHER STITCH

Belonging to the group of looped stitches, feather stitch was widely used for smocking. Similar to blanket stitch, but with the arm of each stitch placed at an angle instead of vertically, the stitches are worked on either side of a central line to create an open, "feathery" appearance. It is particularly useful for covering raw edges and as such is often used in crazy patchwork to cover the joins between the pieces.

Variations

1 Single feather is a slanting buttonhole stitch worked along a straight line.

2 Double feather has extra looped stitches that extend the diagonal lines to create a pronounced zigzag effect.

3 Cretan stitch is a straight-stitched feather stitch variation, which can be used to decoratively cover seams in patchwork.

4, 5 Variations of feather stitch are used to fasten shisha mirrors to the ground fabric.

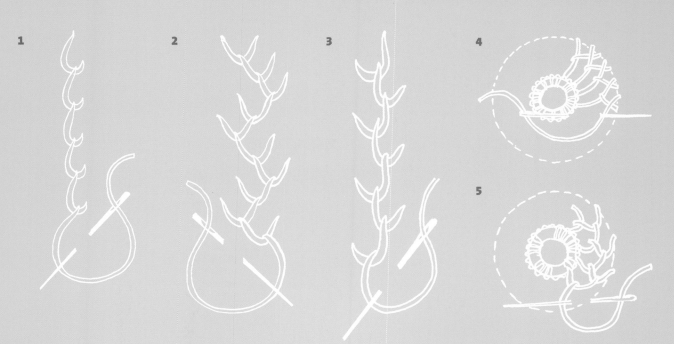

STAR STITCH

This pretty stitch is really a group of four large straight
stitches that are crisscrossed and then tied down with a
smaller cross-stitch at the center. It is very pretty when used
to powder the surface of a fabric, either in an even pattern or
randomly spaced. More often it is used in conjunction with
other stitches to augment a design, as a center for flowers,
or as a circular motif.

THORN STITCH

The name of this stitch is appropriate—it looks exactly like a
twig with straight thorns sticking out of it. It is really a form of
couching (where stitches hold a thread in place), because the
long straight thread (fig 1) is held in position by the shorter
angled threads (fig 2). The variation (fig 3) is worked with the
threads positioned closer together and varying in length so
that leaf shapes can be made with it. By varying the lengths of
the slanting stitches you can make many other undulating
linear patterns with this stitch.

1

2

3

LANE OR LAZY BEADING

This quick method of beading is a form of couching because the beads are strung onto the secured thread (fig 1) then couched down in position with a short stitch between the beads (fig 2). The couching stitches can be worked between every other bead for undulations or curves, or between small numbers of beads for a quicker method.

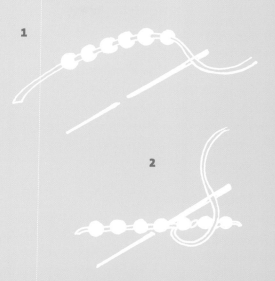

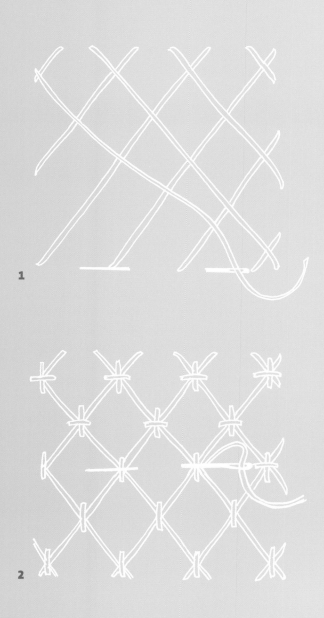

JACOBEAN TRELLIS STITCH

Using this filling pattern is a quick and easy way to cover a large area of fabric with embroidery. In this couching technique, the threads underneath are laid in long lines that crisscross and are held in place with a series of upright cross-stitches.

To work the stitch, lay down a series of parallel threads over the whole area of the pattern to be covered, taking care to measure the spaces between the lines accurately. Stitch another set of lines across the first set, making a trellis (fig 1).

Work a series of upright cross-stitches over the intersections of the trellis threads (fig 2); this secures the whole embroidery in position. It is generally neater and quicker to work the cross-stitches in separate rows, almost like running stitches, rather than to work each stitch individually. This method also ensures that all the top crossed stitches are worked in the same direction, which adds to the fluency of the embroidery.

INSERTION STITCHES

There is a range of useful stitches for drawn-thread work. I use just some of them, which are shown below.

Double border hem stitch

This is really herringbone stitch worked as a drawn-thread stitch. It has many other names, such as herringbone insertion stitch. It is worked over a strip of woven fabric that is left intact after fabric threads have been withdrawn from both sides, leaving a narrow band of solid fabric. The rows of remaining fabric threads are divided into groups that are stitched together in alternating pairs, on each side of the band of intact fabric. A new group of threads is picked up with each stitch, to form a decorative and lacy design.

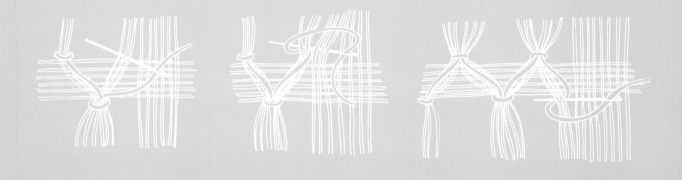

Coral knot insertion stitch

A simple knotted stitch, coral stitch is usually worked as a decorative line, but it can also be used as an insertion stitch to tie together even-numbered groups of fabric threads, to keep them firmly in position in a channel of withdrawn threads. Here the coral knot insertion stitches draw together the fabric threads in clusters of six. This stitch looks neat when viewed from the back, so it is ideal for a scarf, for example, where the reverse side is on view.

Twisted insertion stitch

The common name for this stitch is fagoting, and it is used to join two separate pieces of braid or of hemmed fabrics together, so that a space remains between them. The pretty looped stitch shows clearly between the joins. Use a firm thread and keep an even space between the two edges of fabric being stitched together.

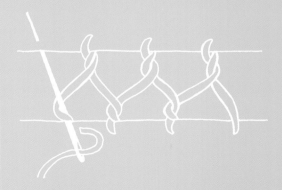

Assembly

While many of the designs in this book can be embroidered on found objects, here are the assembly instructions for items you may want to create yourself, using your own choice of fabrics and colorways.

BEADED BAG

The little beaded evening bag (see page 32) has an embroidered front and handsewn edges.

Using the pattern-piece shape on page 106, cut out the embroidered fabric, leaving the correct seam allowances as marked. Using the same pattern, cut out a piece of lightweight fusible batting and the lining. Press the batting onto the back of the embroidery (fig 1). Place the embroidery and the lining right sides together. Pin and baste, then machine stitch them together all the way around, leaving a small 2" (5-cm) gap in the side of the bag (fig 2). Turn right side out through the gap left in the side seam. Lightly press all the seams on the lining side. Slip stitch the opening to close.

Fold the bag in half, lining sides together, and stitch the sides through the machine stitches: Starting 1½" (3 cm) below the top, stitch to the fold (fig 3). Sew the rings for the handles onto the small shoulders of the bag, using a matching thread (fig 4). Attach the eyeglasses cords.

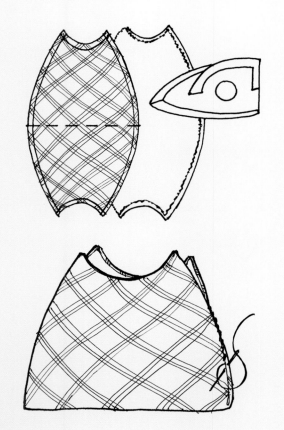

1

3

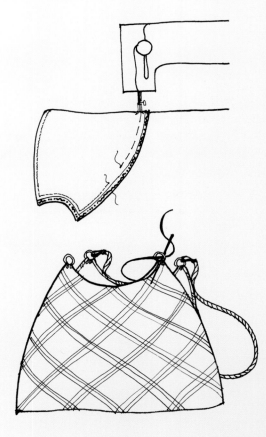

2

4

PICTURE FRAME

The instructions here are for finishing the picture frames on page 58. Cover your cardboard frame as follows:

Place the frame (used to mark the outline of the design) on a piece of batting, and cut the batting to the exact size of the frame (fig 1). Using fabric glue, fix batting in position and let dry.

Place the cardboard frame on the back of the finished embroidery and mark around it with a water-soluble pen or silver fabric-marking pencil. Cut a cross at the center of the embroidery fabric, making the cuts as far into the corners as you dare without cutting any of the beaded embroidery while doing so (fig 2).

Place the frame, padded side down, on the back of the embroidery fabric again. Apply glue to the inside edge and pull the fabric through the hole into position. Make sure that all the fabrics are securely glued in position (fig 3).

Pull the outside edges of the fabric onto the back of the frame and glue these (fig 4). You may need to trim the edges a little first. Start with the top and bottom edges, making sure that these are even by checking that no pen marks are visible on the front. When these two edges are secure, pull the side edges to the back and glue them.

The frame is ready to be assembled according to the manufacturer's instructions.

1

2

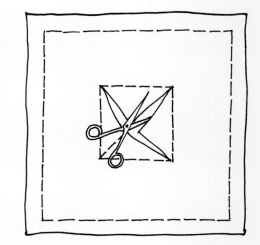

3

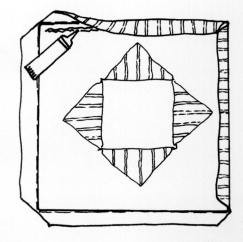

4

PILLOW COVERS

There are two methods for sewing a pillowcover. The instructions for Version 1 are suitable for the flame-stitch pillow on pages 70–71. Those for Version 2 suit the bull's-eye pillow on pages 24–29.

Version 1

Sizes for the canvas front and two fabric back pieces (including a ¾" [2-cm] seam allowance all around) are given in the instructions for the flame-stitch pillow.

Make a ¾" (2-cm) hem along the center edge of each back piece (fig 1). Overlap the two back pieces and place them on top of the embroidered canvas, with the RIGHT sides together. Pin and baste all the way around and machine stitch (fig 2). Trim off the corners close to the stitching line and turn right side out. The pillow form is inserted through the split, so there is no need for any further fastenings.

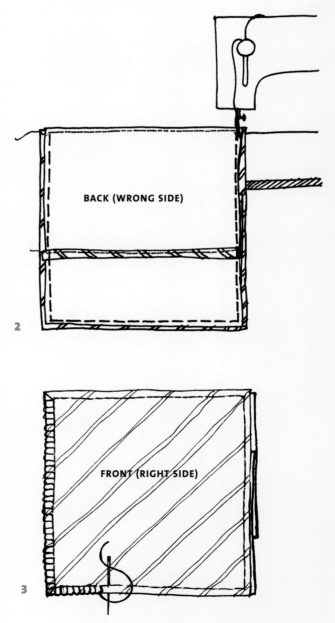

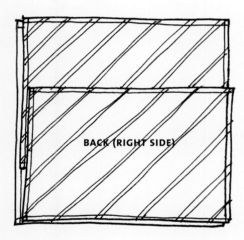

BACK (RIGHT SIDE)

1

BACK (WRONG SIDE)

2

Version 2

There is no need to hem the front and two back pieces of the bull's-eye pillow because felt does not fray. Draw a stitching guideline ½" (1 cm) from the edge with a water-soluble pen, all the way around the appliquéd front. Pin and baste the WRONG sides of the front and back together, overlapping the back pieces. Carefully machine stitch over the guideline using monofilament thread. On the pillow front, blanket stitch the edges with your chosen buttonhole variation (see page 95), using the machine line as a guide for the stitch length (fig 3). Blanket stitch the center edge of the top back piece as well.

FRONT (RIGHT SIDE)

3

CANDLEWICK BOLSTER

The instructions here are for the bolster shown on page 52; it measures 10" (25 cm) in diameter by 36" (90 cm) in length.

Cut one central piece of fabric 32½" x 37" (81 x 97 cm) with the stripes running parallel to the shorter sides. Cut two end pieces 32½" x 6½" (81 x 16 cm) with the stripes running parallel to the shorter sides. When the embroidery is completed, stitch the ends to the central piece and press open the seams (fig 1).

Fold the fabric in half along the length, and pin and baste the seam. Machine stitch the seam but leave a hole through which to thread the gathering cord by double stitching the first ¾" (2 cm) then leaving a gap of ½" (1 cm) before continuing to the end, where the same size gap and double stitching are repeated (fig 2).

At each end of the bolster, turn under ¼" (5 mm) and press. Turn under a ½" (1-cm) hem, large enough to accommodate your cord, and pin and baste in place. Machine stitch around the whole circumference of the pillow (fig 3) and turn right side out. Thread the cord through the gaps in the inside of the channel and pull to close.

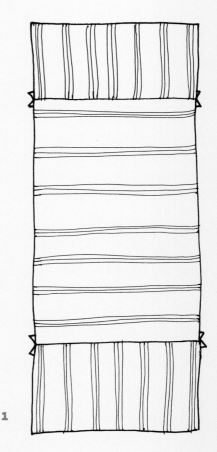

1

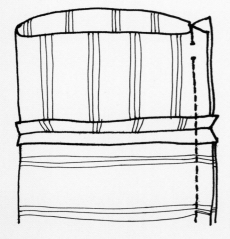

2

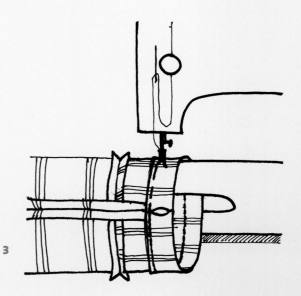

3

CRAZY PATCHWORK BOOK COVER

The instructions for the book cover on page 38 are for a cover big enough for a standard-size folder or a large book.

Trim and hem the narrow ends of the embroidery cover with a double-folded machined hem or a single one that is decoratively buttonhole stitched. Place the embroidered side of the fabric face down and lay the open book on top of it. Fold the ends of the fabric over the open book cover and mark the fold line and top and bottom of the book with a water-soluble pen on the inside of the fabric (fig 1). For a thick book, fold over the fabric with the book closed, and mark the positions (fig 2).

Press the folds, then fold the fabric to the opposite side so that the right sides are together. Machine or backstitch these short seams in position, and snip off the corners close to the stitching line (fig 3).

Turn the cover right side out. Fold under and press the top and bottom edges. Trim off any excess fabric if necessary. Herringbone stitch the hems in place (page 96), being careful not to stitch through to the front of the embroidery (fig 4).

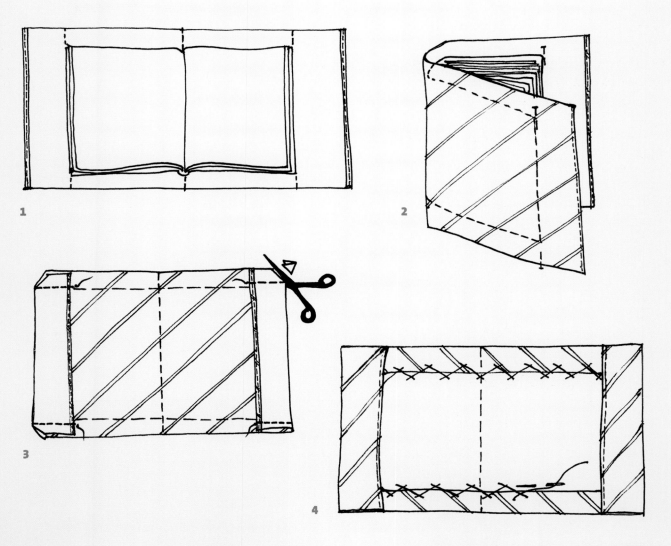

Motifs, patterns, and charts

The charts and motifs required for the projects in this book are shown on the following pages. Check the information with each motif to work out the actual size.

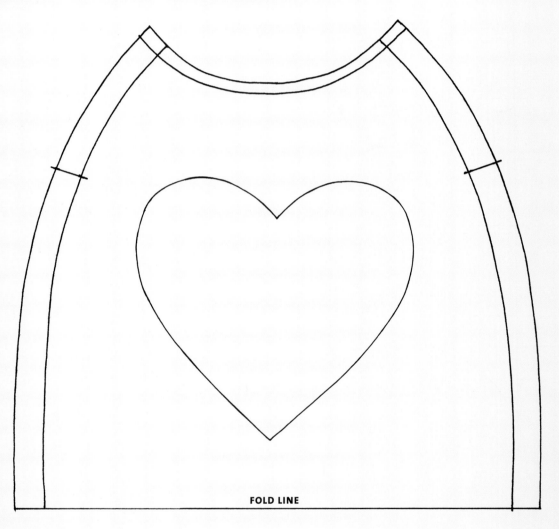

FOLD LINE

BEADED EVENING BAG
(see pages 30–35)
To achieve the actual size for the bag, enlarge the outline above by 70 percent (ignore the heart). Lay the bottom edge on a fold of fabric to cut a single piece for the front and back.

HEART APPLIQUÉ QUILT
(see pages 40–45)
Use the heart motif above for the hearts on the appliqué quilt. Enlarge by 100 percent to achieve the actual size for the motif.

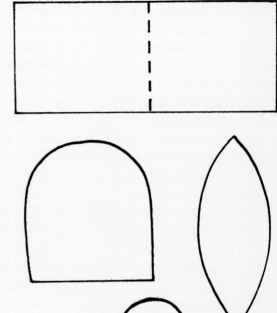

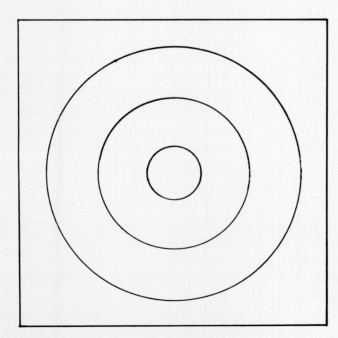

FELT FLOWER BAG

(see pages 74–79)

The diagrams above and above left show the pattern pieces for this design. Enlarge the diagram above left by 330 percent to achieve the actual size. The pieces for the individual flowers above are shown here the actual size.

BULL'S-EYE PILLOW

(see pages 24–29)

The diagrams left are for the four individual patch pieces for this pillow. Enlarge by 46 percent to achieve the actual size for the patches.

FLAME-STITCH PILLOW

(see pages 68–73)

Transfer the design (below) to graph paper; each stitch should cover seven squares of graph paper. Enlarge by 360 percent to achieve the actual size.

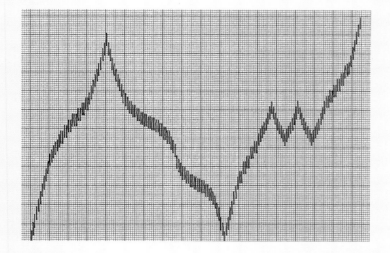

MEXICAN-STYLE ESPADRILLES

(see pages 18–23)

You need the left- and right-foot designs (below) for the pair of shoes. The design is shown here the actual size.

TRADITIONAL FLORAL MOTIF

(see pages 62–67)

Enlarge the rose design (above) by 170 percent to achieve the actual size needed for the project.

SHISHA-MIRROR HAT

(see pages 80–85)

The hat top pattern is shown below; the hat band pattern (right) represents half of hat band. Place the straight short edge on the fold of the fabric to cut the double length. Enlarge the hat top and band by 87 percent to achieve the actual size.

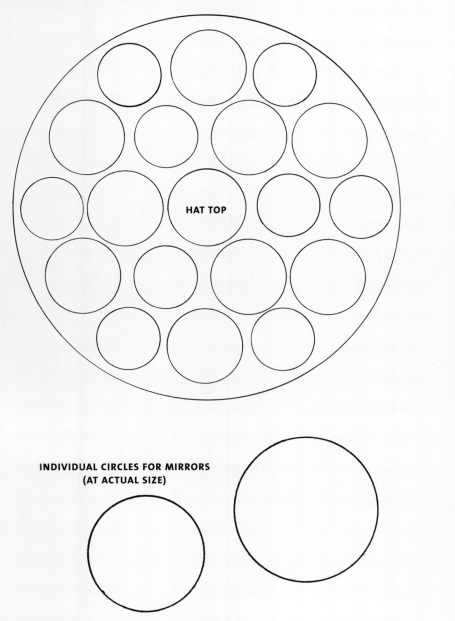

HAT TOP

INDIVIDUAL CIRCLES FOR MIRRORS (AT ACTUAL SIZE)

HAT BAND

Project profiles

The photographs below showcase the principal projects in this book. Some are available as kits from Coats Crafts UK (see Suppliers, opposite). You can find further information about them, and about similar projects and kits from the sister volume to this book, *White on White*, by Janet Haigh, on the Coats Crafts website.

Mexican-style espadrilles, p. 20

Bull's-eye pillow, p. 26

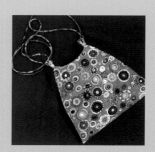

Beaded evening bag, p. 32

Crazy patchwork book cover, p. 38

Appliqué quilt, p. 42

French knot scarf, p. 48

Candlewick bolster, p. 52

Running-stitch frames, p. 58

Traditional floral motif, p. 64

Flame-stitch pillow, p. 70

Felt-flower bag, p. 76

Shisha-mirror hat, p. 82

SUPPLIERS

For the materials used in this book, contact your local craft, needlework, or fabric store or contact the companies below.

Coats and Clark
Consumer Services
P.O. Box 12229
Greenville, South Carolina 29612-0229
(800) 648-1479
www.coatsandclark.com
www.coatscrafts.co.uk

Rowan Yarns Ltd.
Westminster Fibers, Inc.
4 Townsend West, Unit 8
Nashua, New Hampshire 03063
(603) 886-5041
(800) 445-9276
www.personalthreads.com/
westminsterfibers.htm

DMC Corporation
South Hackensack Ave.
Port Kearny Building 10F
South Kearny, New Hampshire 07032
www.dmc.com

Overseas stockists

There are branches of Coats Crafts in most countries. The following are the principal website addresses, but if you wish to find others, check out the main website:

North America: www.coatsandclark.com
India: www.coatsindia.com
Germany:www.coatsgmbh.de/de/1/hme.html
Portugal:www.coatsclark.pt/pt/1/hme.html
Brazil: www.coatscorrente.com.br

Kits

Several of the projects shown in this book are available in kit form. To find out more about them, contact Coats Crafts UK or visit you local crafts store (details of Coats stores throughout the country are listed on the website).

Additional suppliers:

Whaleys (Bradford) Ltd., Harris Courts Great Horton, Bradford, West Yorkshire BD7 4EQ, United Kingdom
e-mail: whaleys@btinternet.com
www.whaleys.bradford.ltd.uk

ACKNOWLEDGMENTS

My thanks go to the many people who contributed to this book: to Susan Berry, my editor and collaborator, and Stephen Sheard, for providing the impetus for this venture; to the marketing and liaison teams, under Donald McMillan at Coats in Darlington and under Kate Buller at Rowan Yarns in Holmfirth, who promptly supplied the many and varied products for the projects.

I am indebted also to Anne Wilson for her elegant design for the book, John Heseltine for his luminous photography, and Sally Harding for her eye for detail on the text.

I am also indebted to my colleague, Hilary Jagger, who kept me and my business alive with her optimism and humor while making projects for the book. Also to Nigel Hurlstone, fellow embroiderer, who helped me to research several new techniques, and was discovered stitching the flame-stitch pillow between courses at a restaurant, to help meet an imminent photo shoot deadline! Katie Phythian, a BA (Hons) embroidery student, who gave me much needed help preparing materials and June Baker-Atkinson, who made props for photography. I am also indebted to Adrian Campbell for the image of the anemones on pages 56 and 60 and to Roy Grange for the wire-haired fox terrier on pages 60 and 61. And last, to my husband, Stephen Jacobson, who kept me sane throughout.

Index